The Toledo Incident of 1925

First Printing
February 2005

No. ___________ of 5000

Library of Congress Cataloguing-in-Publication data
Cox, Ted W., 1947-

The Toledo Incident of 1925: Three days that made history
in Toledo, Oregon / by Ted W. Cox
Includes index
ISBN 0-9760891-0-6

1. Oregon History. 2. Japanese-Americans—Oregon.
3. Japanese-Americans—*Issei*. 4. Civil Rights-Lawsuits. 5. Diversity.
6. Japanese Immigration, U.S. 7. Toledo, Oregon-
History. 8. Portland, Oregon - History. I. Title.

First Printing, February 2005

Book Design by Matt Harrington

Old World Publications
Corvallis, Oregon, U.S.A.
www.oldworldpublications.com

Table of Contents

INTRODUCTION iii
by Stefan Tanaka

ACKNOWLEDGEMENTS vii

PREFACE xiii

LIST OF PICTURES xix

LIST OF FIGURES xxii

LIST OF TABLES xxii

CHAPTER ONE "The Setting" 2
Toledo, Oregon

CHAPTER TWO "The Toledo Boom" 6
1917-1922 Million Dollar Sawmill

CHAPTER THREE "Rumors Begin" 18
1925 Pacific Spruce Corporation plans to hire Japanese crew

CHAPTER FOUR "The Confrontation" 32
1925 Three days that made history in Toledo, Oregon

CHAPTER FIVE "The Aftermath" 62
1925 Tempest in a Teapot

CHAPTER SIX "Going to Trial" 90
1926 The first civil case of its kind to be tried in the United States

CHAPTER SEVEN "The Judgment" 122

APPENDIX A
1884–1924 Japanese Immigration to the United States 134
1911– Japanese Association of Oregon 135
1925– Japanese (*Issei*) in Oregon Sawmills....................136
1926–1952 Civil Rights for Japanese (*Issei*) Resident Aliens by Tim Willis, Attorney-at-law 137

APPENDIX B
Daiichi Takeoka (1882-1954) 144
Iwao Oyama (1887-1952) and *The Oshu Nippo*....................147
George P. Schenck (1867–1945) 148
Rosemary Schenck (1879–1948)....................149
Owen Hart (1902–1986)....................150

APPENDIX C
Copies of original Japanese newspaper articles 154

PEOPLE INDEX 177

SUBJECT INDEX 184

ABOUT THE AUTHOR....................196

Introduction

It is with great pleasure that I write this introduction for Ted Cox's *The Toledo Incident of 1925*. To say the least, I was surprised when he contacted me; it has been over thirty years since I wrote the paper that became the article. Though distant, I have a fondness for that essay; it is my first, and more importantly, it gave me the confidence that I can become a historian.

I thought I had moved to different subjects, from Japanese Americans and labor to modern Japan, time, and history itself. Yet Cox's thoroughly researched account has reminded me why I became involved in this profession and why it is such a pleasure to research, practice, and write history. In past events, people have done both the great and not-so-great things, and through them we try to understand better our current situations. All too often, it seems that most of the fundamental issues remain.

The Toledo Incident shows that we all need both a respect for and humility toward history. Our knowledge of the past is never as accurate as we think. History constantly changes and is never complete. On the one hand, we don't always understand the myriad connections (our own histories) that frame our lives. Cox demonstrates how local events are rarely really local in modern society. They are tied to broader national and international conditions. In 1925, Toledo was caught up in the national economy: The mill was a result of the new technology—airplanes—and the demand for spruce. Internationally, the 1911 Treaty of Commerce and Navigation was used by *Issei* to ensure their rights as legal aliens. What for the supporters of the Lincoln County Protective League was a simple question of defending their idea of community was in essence tied to national and international political and economic issues.

On the other hand, the categories that guide us (another form of history) are usually partial at best. The argument against the Japanese centered on ideas of race, more specifically "Orientals," that have a long history and are too familiar in confrontations involving race and ethnicity: they would bring lower wages and a decline of the standard of the community. As today, race, morals, ethics, religion, etc. are ideas that too frequently are used to amplify differences and foster a dislike for others because of their perceived alienness, without recognizing how similar individuals are, usually against some corporate or national interests. Why have such ideas remained so powerful?

Recent and the best historical research has shown that such emotional and naturalized categories like race, gender, religion, sexual orientation did not have the same meaning in the pre-modern past (no matter how natural we consider them today). What we think we know was not so earlier. Here, we should be skeptical toward our inherited knowledge and try to understand people as individuals, not as categories. The lament of the *Great Northern Daily News* was insightful; weren't the interests of the mill workers and the Japanese workers more similar vis-à-vis the Corporation?

This event is an early example of the problems that emerge in what we today call globalization, and there are many books examining the impact of globalization on local communities. Properly, the District Court in Portland did not exonerate such acts as the expulsion of the Japanese; but what responsibilities do corporations such as the Pacific Spruce Corporation have? Should they also be citizens of the community in which they are located. In Cox's balanced account, this event suggests that it was (is) not considered necessary: the mill disregarded the sentiment of the town, and *Issei* went to Toledo only after receiving assurances from the mill. This is the difficulty of today's increasingly global and corporatized world. Economically based decisions are acceptable. The question is not how a corporation fits into a community, but whether the community can support a corporation.

But this does not mean that our lives are completely circumscribed (I hope). Instead, this account demonstrates that history consists of stories about how individuals act when faced with the unexpected. Despite our attempts to control, even sanitize, our immediate world, we confront unexpected situations. The lives of the Japanese, Filipinos, and Korean were no doubt affected by this event. The decisions that they made at the moment, and especially later in deciding to file lawsuits affected the status of Japanese Americans. On the other side, a young man, Owen Hart, playing in the ball field, allowed himself to get swept up in the frenzy, a decision he regretted for years. One cannot help but ask how we would act today if faced with such events. This, too, is history.

Finally, I am especially pleased that Cox is retrieving a part of the history of the first generation of Japanese in the United States. The history of Japanese Americans has developed a great deal since the *Pacific Northwest Quarterly* published my essay in 1978. Yet most of that history is about the terrible incarceration of the Japanese Americans during World War II, and about the forbearance and loyalty of the *Nisei* in pointing out to the rest of the United States its mistaken notions of race—especially toward Japanese Americans. The history of the first generation has not received similar attention.

When we look at these pioneers, we see struggle, fortitude, and a fight for rights. The phrase "shikata ga nai" (it can't be helped) does not exist in this incident; certainly not in the lawsuits filed. This incident, like other parts of the history of *Issei,* tells us about another part of the past of Japanese Americans, one that has until recently been overshadowed.

Stefan Tanaka
San Diego, California
December 21, 2004

Acknowledgements

I am grateful to many individuals and organizations that helped in the writing of this book.

My involvement in Toledo began in 1977 when I started making weekly trips from Corvallis in the Willamette Valley to the Oregon coast with my friend Roy Green who turned ninety-five years old in 2005. Roy was born in Missouri in 1910 and lived in Toledo from 1922 to 1952. Over the last twenty-eight years, Roy and I have discussed the large and small events in his life, including "the Japanese story." These conversations prompted me to keep an eye out for information about Toledo's history.

In 1995 Lincoln County historian Mike O'Donnell wrote an article about the Japanese deportation in the *Newport News-Times*. The article answered some of my questions about the expulsion. Five years later Steve M. Wyatt, former curator of the Oregon Coast History Center, also wrote about the incident in *The Bayfront Magazine*. By that time I was planning to write Roy Green's biography and after reading Wyatt's article, I considered researching and writing about the Toledo Incident because the riot and resulting trial was such a compelling story.

In 2002, thanks to research friend Betty McNally, I came across an on-line book about Lincoln County history written by Connie Guardino, a former Toledo resident who had compiled considerable information that gave a good understanding about the deportation.

Then an essay published in the *Pacific Northwest Quarterly* came to my attention. "The Toledo Incident: The Deportation of the *Nikkei* from an Oregon Mill Town" was written by fourth generation Japanese American Stefan Tanaka and published in 1978. He is currently Professor of History at the University of California, San Diego and author of two books, *Japan's Orient: Rendering Past Into History* and *New Times in Modern Japan*. His essay on the Toledo Incident is the most thorough and well-documented work written on the topic to date. The article has been used as a reference in other historical writings; I used his essay to springboard into my own research for information.

At the time I decided to write a biography of Roy Green's life in Toledo, the Japanese deportation story was going to be one chapter among many. With a draft of Roy's biography in hand, I met with John Baker, author of *Camp Adair*, to get his impressions on how he thought Roy's story was coming along. He brought out the idea that the Toledo Incident really needed to stand on its own.

At my son's wedding, in the summer of 2003, I struck up a conversation with John Uggen, Spanish Professor and Chair at Willamette University. I explained to John that I was having trouble finding records about the civil trial that followed the Japanese eviction from Toledo. I also told him I didn't think the court records survived. He assured me that the records did exist, that I just hadn't found the source. That thought encouraged me to keep looking. Five days later I contacted the National Archives-Pacific AK Region in Seattle, Washington, and found the documents I'd been looking for. These archives hold the depositions and the follow-up of the 1926 lawsuit brought against the Toledo deportation leaders. I ordered copies of all of these records, which provided a considerable amount of primary source information.

An important reference in my research came from a report written by the Portland Council of Churches in response to the deportation just three weeks after the 1925 incident.

They had conducted a hearing on the matter shortly after the expulsion occurred. At that meeting, a committee of five was appointed to investigate the incident on behalf of the council. The committee spent considerable time interviewing people involved and gathering information about the deportation. The Council's goals were threefold: to give a "chronology of events," present an "interpretation of more or less intangible facts which have been subject to dispute," and provide "constructive recommendations." The report they produced was thoughtful, well-written and added critical historical insight into what, how and why the deportation occurred. Their findings were published in the *Oregon Voter* on September 12, 1925, and I have found their work to be an excellent resource.

Newspaper accounts were another valuable source of information. Newspapers can be a minefield of biased views and incorrect reporting, but they also can offer a raw insight into events as they occurred—sometimes reflecting perspectives that would be considered politically incorrect by modern-day standards. Fortunately, for my purposes, the Toledo Incident was covered by a variety of newspapers including one surviving *Issei* newspaper from Seattle, Washington, *The Great Northern Daily News (Taihoku Nippo)* which I found in the University of Washington Libraries, Special Collections.

Translations of several copies of the *Great Northern Daily News* were made possible through the efforts of two sets of translators, Mr. Eiji Takemura from the prefecture of Ehime, island of Shikoku, Japan, and Glen-Paul Amick and his wife Mrs. Hiroko Takada Amick, professional translators living in Corvallis, Oregon. My thanks go to these individuals for providing translations of these important documents.

In October 1928, the Oregon Bureau of Labor, through the cooperation of the Japanese Association of Oregon, compiled and published a census of the Japanese population living in

Oregon at that time. Mr. Yorisada Matsui, an *Issei* (first generation Japanese American) contractor, was secretary of the Japanese Association of Oregon and was invaluable in making the census an accurate record. This document provided information on some of the *Issei* men and women discussed in this book.

In April 2004, I approached June Schumann at the Oregon *Nikkei* Legacy Center (Japanese Cultural Center) in Portland for help with my research. Mrs. Schumann suggested that I contact *Nisei* (second generation Japanese American) elder Homer Yasui, M.D., to explain what I was doing. When I called, he immediately took me under his wing, and along with his wife Miki, opened the door to my appreciation of Japanese American history. Homer helped in the research and contacted two *Nisei* elders whose fathers played important roles in the 1926 Toledo Incident lawsuit: Kay Takeoka, D.D.S., and Albert Oyama, M.D.. Homer also located Stefan Tanaka who was previously mentioned in this acknowledgement. I made contact with Tanaka and he agreed to look over a very rough draft of the manuscript. Knowing that he has a busy schedule, I was extremely pleased with this courtesy. In November 2004, he agreed to write the introduction of this book, a gesture for which I will always be grateful. My sincere thanks go to these individuals for their important contributions to the writing of this book.

Roy Green, who was fifteen years old in 1925, introduced me to a number of Toledo elders over the years. Some of them shared what they remembered and had heard about the events of 1925. Jackie Robeson, a lifelong Toledoite was a big supporter of my book and continually encouraged me during its writing. The late Larry Hart and his wife LaRue brought out family records and discussed insights into how the events affected their family. I talked with Pat Dye who shared her childhood memories and photographs for use in telling this story. Earl Roberts, Guy Hendrix, Sid Neal and

Lewis Powers, who were all children living in Toledo in 1925, had comments about the incident which they shared with me. Rolland "Pug" Hart went over a rough draft of the book. Among his comments was the correction of his uncle's name. Monte Boggs, who was born in Toledo, remembered comments made by his father, who was working at the Pacific Spruce Mill at the time the incident occurred. My thanks go out to all of these people for their kindness and support.

Connie Guardino, a writer in her own right, interviewed Harry Hawkins about the incident in the 1970s and has kindly given permission to quote Hawkins' comments in this book.

Celeste Mathews, Events Coordinator for the City of Toledo and third generation Toledoite, shared information, listened and provided important leads for interviews. Thank you, Celeste.

During the writing of this book, Roy and I spent a lot of time at the Timbers Restaurant in downtown Toledo drinking coffee and asking for comments from Toledo folks. The restaurant crew was always interested and supportive; my heartfelt thanks to Rosa Mendoza and all the staff.

Thanks also to Peter Rayment, Lisa Miller, Andrea Haller, and the rest of the staff at the Toledo Public Library for their assistance.

The staff at the Oregon Coast History Center in Newport continued to be helpful throughout the writing and research process. They provided critical articles and photographs necessary to make this book accurate and interesting. Particular thanks go to Loretta Harrison, Executive Director, for supporting my efforts to publish this story, and Jodi Weeber, Museum Registrar, for helping me with my research.

C.D. Johnson, III, was kind enough to talk with me about his father, grandfather, and the green-chain operations at the mill. Thank you Mr. Johnson for letting me into your home.

Tim Willis, an attorney in Corvallis, Oregon, provided legal advice and interpretation of the significance of the 1926 trial. He wrote the section on civil rights and the *Issei* in Appendix A and made valuable comments about Daiichi Takeoka in Appendix B. I am grateful to Tim for explaining the judicial aspects to me and for his part in writing this book.

Suzannah Doyle worked on both editing and organizing the promotion of this book. Thank you Suzannah for letting me tap into your knowledge and for all the brainstorming we did.

Matt Harrington, Graphic Designer for the City of Albany, Oregon, did the final layout and design for the book. Thank you Matt for your graphic wizardry.

Melissa Román gave editorial comments in organizing and focusing my ideas. I incorporated her rewrite suggestions into my work. Without her help, I wouldn't have finished the manuscript in a timely fashion. Thank you Melissa for teaching me so much about writing.

Betty McNally provided invaluable sources used to pull the bits and pieces of this story together. Thank you, Betty, for your research skills.

My sister-in-law, Linda Rehn, spent considerable time editing rough drafts for which I am extremely grateful. Thank you Linda for taking the time to read, comment and suggest.

Some, but not all, of the other people involved in this project include: Matt Amano, Roy Bennett, Lynne Chandler, Chris Coffin, Ray Currier, Dixie Francis, Lauren Kessler, Martha Jenkins, Mary Johnson, Simon Johnson's senior citizen's writing class, Judy Rycraft Juntunen, Nik Matsler, Cheri McLain, Janet O'Day, Lloyd M. Palmer, Sandy Smith, Linda Tamura, Tom Weller, Joan Wessell, Marcus Widenor, Jack Wolcott and Terry Woolfolk. Thank you all for your individual contributions.

A very special thank you goes to my wife, Veronica, who still welcomes me through the door after my time away researching and writing this book.

Preface

On July 12, 1925, a predominantly Caucasian mob of about fifty men (urged on by over two hundred women and children), forced a group of Japanese laborers and their families to leave Toledo, Oregon. The following year in 1926, a federal circuit court in Portland, Oregon, delivered a civil verdict against five of the Toledo residents involved in the expulsion. These five people received a stiff financial penalty for violating the Japanese laborers' civil rights.

Just after the 1925 incident, newspapers from around Oregon expressed outrage over the expulsion. However, if the same incident had occurred three years earlier, public response would probably have been indifference. Likewise, had the 1926 civil trial been held in 1922, there is a good chance that few juries in the state would have found in favor of the Japanese. How could such a different response been possible if the incident had occurred just three years earlier?

In 1894, a U.S. circuit court ruled that Japanese immigrants were ineligible for naturalization because they were neither Black nor White but Mongolian. The court declared that the Japanese immigrants were "Aliens ineligible for citizenship."[1] However, this ruling did not stop Japanese immigration to the United States. From 1900 to 1925, Oregon's Japanese resident population including their American born children increased from twenty-five hundred to over four thousand individuals.[2]

In 1904, the Oregon State Federation of Labor in line with the American Federation of Labor (AFL) called for restrictions on Japanese employment.[3] This labor organization did not want Japanese residents to participate in the American labor movement. The attitude at that time was that Japanese residents should not be naturalized nor unionized. The AFL continued this policy of racial ostracism for over thirty years.[4] Japanese residents did however, form their own guilds and associations, and followed standards set by mainstream unions.[5] In 1907 the Oregon Bureau of Labor [Today called the Oregon Bureau of Labor and Industries) advocated restrictions on Japanese immigration, suggesting that the Japanese immigrants were bringing a lower standard of living into the state.[6]

Following World War I, a national movement to halt Japanese immigration into the United States was mounting. At the same time in Oregon, there was pressure to restrict Japanese residents from owning or leasing land. Oregon state legislators referred to Japanese immigrants as "threatening American values."[7] This climate of discrimination was fueled by perceptions that Japanese immigrants would not assimilate into the nation's social fabric and that they would overrun the west coast taking land and jobs away from Caucasians.[8]

From the Japanese resident perspective, they were willing to work hard, sacrifice and save for a better future. They had an attitude that exemplified the puritan work ethic of the dominant culture. Oregon author Lauren Kessler commented that the Japanese immigrant; "practiced the protestant work ethic with an intensity that overwhelmed their white neighbors...they were the new puritans, and the old puritans didn't like it."[9] Like so many other immigrant Americans, the Japanese were working hard to build for themselves and their children a better life in this country.

Oregon State Senator W.W. Banks was one lone voice in the Oregon legislature who spoke in support of the Japanese immigrant in 1921. He pointed out that they had an exemplary record while living in the state and that they posed no threat to the Caucasian majority. The following year he was defeated in a bid for re-election.[10]

In 1921 the Ku Klux Klan established a presence in Oregon and rapidly found its way to all levels of society.[11] The Klan entered the state under a banner of moral improvement and one hundred percent Americanism. It was a mainstream movement, recruiting police, elected officials, businessmen, factory workers, clerks, dentists, storeowners, etc. Within a year there were fourteen thousand Klan members statewide with one of the highest per-capita memberships in the country.[12] In 1922 the Klan influenced state government by giving support to the successful election of Governor Walter M. Pierce and support to a majority of candidates that got elected to the Oregon House of Representatives.[13]

In 1923, three laws were passed in Oregon directed against the Japanese immigrant.[14] The following year the United States Congress passed the 1924 Immigration Act. Among other things, the new federal law prohibited the immigration of Japanese to the United States. Min Yasui, Oregon's first Japanese American lawyer, commented on the impact of this law; "This Federal Act prevented the reunion of husband and wife, brother and sister, parents and children. . .in numerous ways they (Japanese immigrant) were made to feel that they were neither desired nor respected."[15] These state and federal laws amounted to public-sanctioned discrimination. It was an intensive time for the Japanese, some of whom had already made Oregon their home for over twenty years.

After the federal and state laws were in place, agitation against Japanese residents seems to have subsided.[16] The fears held by many Caucasian Americans that Japanese immigrants were economic and social threats were less intense. It was as if the majority did not feel such a need to draw the racial line emotionally because they had drawn the line legally. At this point in time the Toledo Incident takes place. The incident led to a federal civil lawsuit the following year. The verdict, favoring the Japanese, established federal legal protection for minorities in the work force. It also sent a warning that mob violence, like that which occured in Toledo the previous year, would not be tolerated without stiff financial penalty.

I have used the terms Japanese immigrant and Japanese resident interchangeably so far in this preface. Both terms refer to Japanese aliens living legally in the United States. Since so much of this story centers on the Japanese immigrant community, there are three key terms that the reader should know.

Issei (Pronounced EE-Say) refers to Japanese immigrants who came to the United States in significant numbers from 1884 to 1924. In 1924 Japanese immigration was virtually halted by federal law.

Throughout this book, the terms Japanese resident, Japanese immigrant, Japanese, and *Issei* are used interchangeably.

Nisei (Pronounced NEE-say) are Japanese American children of *Issei*; they are the second generation. Born U.S. citizens, *Nisei* grew up with the same rights and entitlements under the law given any U.S. national.

As part of their cultural identity, the Japanese American community is referred to as *Nikkei* (pronounced Nee-Kay). The terms *Issei*, *Nisei* and *Nikkei* signify a culture that has adapted to the melting pot of America while still retaining their own identity.

One question that often arises when I talk to people about this story is whether the *Issei* who came to work for the Pacific Spruce Corporation in 1925 had arrived directly from Japan. None had. In fact the three children were actually *Nisei* and all others had been for some time *Issei*. The majority were residents of Oregon, some of whom had lived in the state for over 20 years. These individuals held alien resident status, allowing them to legally live and work in the United States. Unlike European immigrants, Japanese immigrants were not allowed to become American citizens until 1952.

Another question involves the relationship between the Toledo Incident and World War II. There is no relationship. However, the anger directed against the Japanese in Toledo did fuel anti-American sentiment in Japan in 1925.

History includes the best and worst of human nature. When recounting the past, there is often the temptation to sidestep the more uncomfortable actions and remember only the good that people do. However, we are the sum of all of our actions. By studying all of the aspects of the events behind us, both good and bad, we can have a better understanding of our past and our present.

Ted W. Cox
Corvallis, Oregon
February 2005

NOTES

[1]Chuman, Frank, *The Bamboo People: The Law and Japanese Americans,* (Del Mar, CA, Publishers Inc., 1976), 67.

[2]Oregon Bureau of Labor, *Census: Japanese Population in Oregon*, (Salem, Oregon, October 1, 1928). Tamura, Linda. "Railroads, Stumps, and Sawmills: Japanese Settlers of the Hood River Valley." *Oregon Historical Quarterly,* (Winter 1993-94): 370.

[3]Johnson, Daniel P. "Anti-Japanese Legislation in Oregon, 1917-1923." *Oregon Historical Quarterly*, (Summer 1996): 178.

[4]Yuji, Ichioka, *The Issei: The World of the First Generation Japanese Immigrants, 1885-1924*, (New York:The Free Press, 1988),102.

[5]Azuma, Eiichiro. "A History of Oregon's Issei, 1880-1952," *Oregon Historical Quarterly* (Winter 1993-94): 333.

[6]Johnson, 178.

[7]Johnson, 194.

[8]Johnson, 183.

[9]"Editor's Introduction." *Oregon Historical Quarterly*, (Winter

1993-94): 309.

[10]Johnson, 196.

[11]"Klan Meets at Salem," *Morning Oregonian*, 30 January 1926. The Klan had about twenty-five chapters throughout Oregon in 1925, but was losing popularity due to corruption and internal fighting. By the end of the decade there were very few members left.

[12]The Oregonian. *The Oregon Story 1850-2000*. (Portland, Oregon: Graphic Arts Center Publishing Company, 2000): 48.

[13]Johnson, 197.

[14]Johnson, 199.

[15]"We, Too, Please, Are 100 Per Cent Americans," Sunday Oregonian, 4 February 1940.

[16]Johnson, 177.

List of Pictures

No.	Caption	Page
1.	2004–aerial view of Toledo. Toledo proper sits on the hill at the center of the photograph.	2
2.	The road curving from the right at the center of the photograph is the Hwy. 20 Business Bypass. The road leading to the left goes to Newport, following along the Yaquina River.	4
3.	1918–DeHaviland Bi-Plane. Northwest spruce was the preferred material for building the observation bi-plane.	6
4.	Toledo waterfront, 1918. The soldier tent camp and the new spruce mill under construction lay beyond the storefronts and across Depot Slough on the "island."	10
5.	The Fir and Spruce Lumber Company, as pictured above in 1911, had changed its name briefly to the Yaquina Bay Railroad and Lumber Company in 1918.	11
6.	This full page advertisement appeared in the July 17, 1919, *Morning Oregonian*.	12
7.	Eastward view of the mill complex.	14
8.	1923–Green-chain line. This sorting line was one of two five hundred foot long sorting areas. Both sorting areas had three moving chains.	19
9.	November 3, 1932, campaign advertisement.	20
10.	1923–A group of men waiting for dinner at the Pacific Spruce Cafeteria.	24
11.	An advertisement in the 1924 Toledo Telephone Directory.	24

No.	Caption	Page
12.	C. Dean Johnson, III, standing by a picture of his father Dean Johnson. September 30, 2004.	24
13.	Passenger train leaves Toledo on its way to Yaquina City August 27, 1918. Background buildings include the *Lincoln County Leader* on the left and Yaquina Bay Railroad and Lumber Company.	32
14.	This 1925 picture shows the construction of the Japanese housing complex in the center foreground of the photograph.	33
15.	Tamakichi Ogura is standing on the left. Ichiro Kawamoto, foreman, is standing on the right. Photograph was taken in July 1926 in Portland, Oregon.	34
16.	George Schenck was a member of the Toledo Police Force for seventeen years. Photograph was taken July 1926 in Portland, Oregon.	35
17.	The Toledo Baseball Field as it looked in 2004.	36
18.	1924–Public Meeting at the Toledo Baseball Field.	37
19.	1927–Harry Hawkins in the Second Grade.	39
20.	Photograph of Mamie Altree as she appeared in the 1910s.	40
21.	2002–aerial view. The white arrows indicate the route to and from Tokyo Slough taken by the mob on July 12, 1925.	42
22.	Tokyo Slough in 2004. Shed Five located middle right above is used today (2004) for storage and railroad car wood chip dumping.	43
23.	C.D. Johnson in 1923. He was deputized the day before the 1925 riot.	44
24.	Dean Johnson in 1923. He was deputized the day before the 1925 riot.	44
25.	Owen Hart, circa 1928.	45
26.	Frank W. Stevens in 1923. He was deputized the night before the 1925 riot.	45

No.	Caption	Page
27.	Tokyo Slough in 1926. The Japanese housing located is in the center foreground of the picture.	47
28.	Deputy Markham's handgun that was dredged from Tokyo Slough.	49
29.	1923–Pacific Spruce office building.	51
30.	*The Great Northern Daily News* was published six days a week.	65
31.	This photograph was taken in 1951, the year before Mr. Iwao Oyama died.	73
32.	The *Oregon News* Logo–Portland, Oregon 1938.	73
33.	Today the League of Women Voters® publishes the *Oregon Voter*.	76
34.	Copy of Summons delivered in Toledo, Oregon, October 2, 1925.	78
35.	(Charles) Daiichi Takeoka. Family portrait taken circa 1915.	81
36.	Affidavit of Ichiro Kawamoto signed by Daiichi Takeoka.	82
37.	Photograph taken on the courthouse steps in Portland during the 1926 trial. In the center, front row, are George Schenck, his son Jack Schenck, and Rosemary Schenck.	91
38.	Although charges were dropped against Buck, his name went through the court process as can be seen on this verdict filing.	122
39.	1913–Oregana yearbook graduation picture, University of Oregon.	144
40.	Taken from newspaper dated April 15, 1938.	146
41.	June Schumann in front of the Merchant Hotel building, October 28, 2004. She is holding a copy of the *Oregon News* dated April 15, 1938.	147
42.	An Advertisement in the August 31, 1900, *Lincoln County Leader.*	148

List of Figures

No.	Caption	Page
A.	1923–Newport-Toledo Map. The Yaquina River was a major transportation route for both people and wood products for many years. The distance betweeen Newport and Toledo by river is approximately 11 miles.	3
B.	1918–Toledo sawmills and the 65-plus acre industrial area known as the "island". In 1923 an additional seven acres was purchased on the "island".	9
C.	1925–Layout of the Pacific Spruce Sawmill and surrounding area	30

List of Tables

Table		Page
1.	Toledo Population Table	13
2.	Brief biographies of the Plaintiffs.	77
3.	Lincoln County Grand Jury, 1926	84
4.	Japanese Mill Employees	137

Chapter I: The Setting

Toledo, Oregon

Founded in 1866, Toledo sits eleven miles up the Yaquina River from the central Oregon coast. Built on a small hill with surrounding tidelands, the town is wrapped by Depot Slough to the north, Olalla Slough to the east and the Yaquina River to the west (Photograph 1). The three bodies of water around Toledo average eight feet above sea level but rise and fall by up to nine feet every six hours due to the ocean tide. High and low tides in Toledo are about thirty minutes later than high and low tides along the coast.[1]

Movement along the Yaquina River was vital to the economic development of Toledo. As the timber industry

Photograph by Ted W. Cox—2004

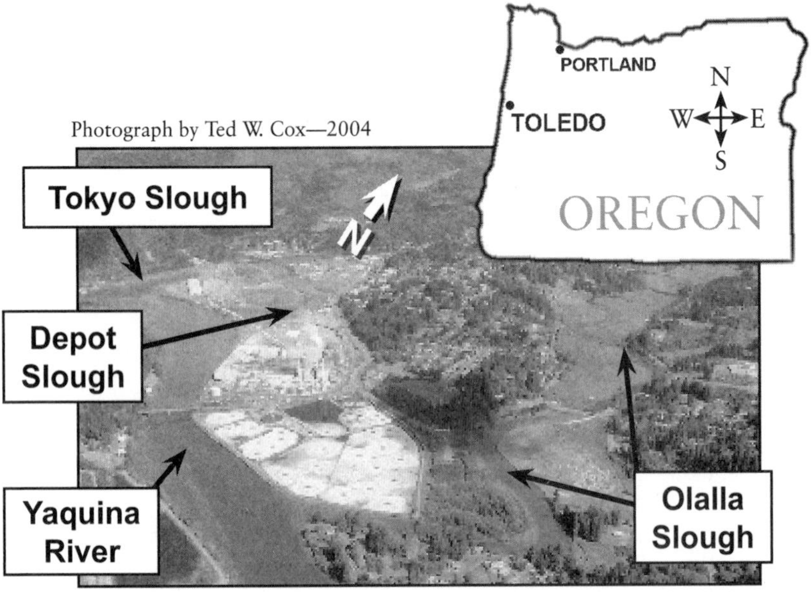

1. 2004–aerial view of Toledo. Toledo proper sits on the hill at the center of the photograph.

Map courtesy of Lincoln County Historical Society, Newport, Oregon

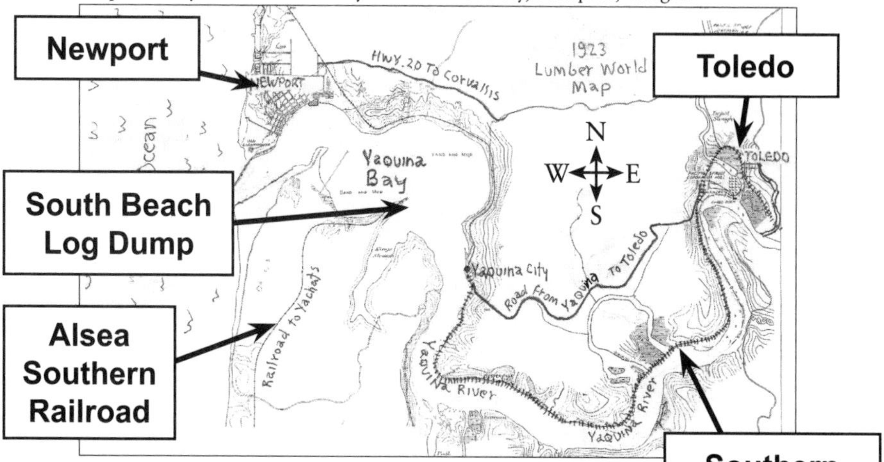

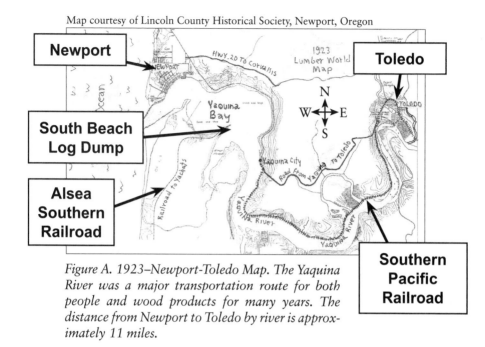

Figure A. 1923–Newport-Toledo Map. The Yaquina River was a major transportation route for both people and wood products for many years. The distance from Newport to Toledo by river is approximately 11 miles.

developed in Lincoln County, the power of the ocean tide made the river extremely important for moving log rafts from Newport to Toledo. For example, from 1922 to 1936 the Alsea Southern Railroad from Yachats to Newport dumped logs into Yaquina Bay at South Beach. Logs were then tied together into "rafts" that were later moved by tugboat along the river with the incoming tide (Figure A).

The Toledo industrial area lies at the base of the hill in Photograph 1. The pulp and paper mill aeration ponds sit in the foreground of the photograph, and in the background is the area known as Tokyo Slough (or Little Tokyo), so named since 1925 when the Pacific Spruce Corporation built housing there for Japanese resident laborers brought in to work. Tokyo Slough (Photograph 2) became the genesis for a precedent-setting court battle, ignited when a group of Toledo citizens decided they didn't want a Japanese labor force in their community and made them get out of town.

Photograph by Ted W. Cox - 2004

2. The road curving from the right at the center of the photograph is the Hwy. 20 Business Bypass.[2] *The road leading to the left goes to Newport following along the Yaquina River.*

NOTES

1. Depot Slough and Olalla Slough are river tributaries of the Yaquina River. Tokyo Slough is a shallow inlet (See page 30).

2. At the time of publication, the street referenced in this chapter was named the Highway 20 Business Bypass. The City of Toledo now maintains this street and may consider a name change.

Chapter 2:
The Toledo Boom

1917-1922
Million-Dollar Sawmill

The United States entered the First World War in April 1917. At that time military analysts predicted that the conflict would continue for two to five more years.[1] With the two-to-five-year scenario in mind, military planners believed that air power would play a decisive role in defeating the Germans,[2] and warplanes were used for the first time in history. The allies wanted to build thousands of airplanes for their military forces to use as quickly as possible (Photograph 3).[3]

Since these early warplanes were constructed of wood, the allies needed a rich supply of timber for airplane production. Sitka Spruce was the most likely material. As a durable, light-

Photograph courtesy of Lincoln County Historical Society, Newport, Oregon

3. 1918–DeHaviland bi-plane. Northwest spruce was the preferred material for building the observation bi-plane.[4]

weight wood with strong, long fibers, spruce would not splinter if hit by rifle bullets.[5] Sitka Spruce is native along the coasts of Northern California, Oregon, Washington, British Columbia and Alaska. However, the highest concentration of quality straight-grained Sitka grew in two locations: Lincoln County, Oregon and Clallam County, Washington.[6]

In 1917, United States Congress created the Aircraft Production Board under the Council of National Defense.[7] This was followed by the formation of the Spruce Production Division commanded by General Brice P. Disque of the U.S. Army.

Local historian Lloyd M. Palmer had the following comments about the Spruce Production Division:

> In order for the Army to be able to produce the amount of spruce lumber suddenly in demand, Disque began sending thousands of soldiers into the forests of Oregon and Washington. They were located in about 240 camps up and down the coast. For the most part, these camps were between Port Angeles, WA and Coos Bay, OR. Several of the camps were farther inland to facilitate other logging activities. Eventually there would be over 30,000 of these "soldier" loggers of which about 3,000 went to work in Lincoln County.[8]

During March and April 1918, several loads of airplane stock were sent by railroad from the Yaquina Bay Railroad and Lumber Company in Toledo to France.[9] At the same time there was a large government sawmill operating in Vancouver, Washington that was producing one-and-a-half million board feet of airplane quality lumber per day.[10] The Vancouver sawmill cut over fifty percent of the total airplane stock from Oregon and Washington in 1918. During one seven-day period alone, sixty railroad cars loaded with split old growth spruce logs were sent from Lincoln County to the Vancouver mill.[11]

Great Britain, France, Italy[12] and the United States built thousands of warplanes from this northwest spruce with the cost of spruce production shared among the four countries. In 1918 U.S. legislators authorized the creation of the international United States Spruce Corporation to coordinate funding. The United States was the major stockholder.[13]

General Disque realized that preparing airplane spruce for shipment would be more efficient if a sawmill was located closer to where the trees were harvested. In Lincoln County, Toledo proved to be the best location. The town already had three sawmills located just outside the city limits: Yaquina Bay Railroad and Lumber Company, located to the north of the commercial port dock; Guy Roberts Sawmill, located south of the commercial port dock[14] and Chesley Sawmill, built on the old Altree Sawmill property west of town.[15] Yet because of the large quantity of lumber needed to build the warplanes, it was decided that none of the three Toledo sawmills could meet the government's needs. In May the decision was made to build a huge government cut-up mill on a sixty-five plus acre "island" of recently reclaimed tideland (Figure B).[16]

Construction of the new mill was well underway in the summer of 1918 (Photograph 4). When completed, the mill would be capable of producing up to seven hundred fifty thousand board feet of airplane stock per day.[17] Thousands of soldiers were needed to meet this goal. Some were cutting lumber, others were felling trees. Some were building roads, while others worked on laying down railroad ties. The Spruce Division also contracted to hire a large body of civilian employees to fill out crews and work with the soldiers.

The dominance of the military throughout Lincoln County must have been very exciting to those living in the area in 1918, as indicated from the following Toledo newspaper editorial written in July:

> It is estimated that there are approximately 3,000 soldiers in this county at the present time engaged in railroad building, logging and saw milling, but primarily all are

> working to increase the spruce production.
>
> For the past three weeks these khaki-clad laborers have been arriving at the rate of 100 per day, and soldiers camps dot the coastline of Lincoln County from Otter Rock to its southern terminus.
>
> When the Hun is licked, the work that is being done there now as a war measure, will aid in the development and growth of our county.[18]

Although the war effort was on everyone's mind, people were also aware of the impact the military's efforts would have on the future of Lincoln County, considering how the county was benefiting from the improvements underway by the Spruce

Map courtesy of Lincoln County Historical Society, Newport, Oregon

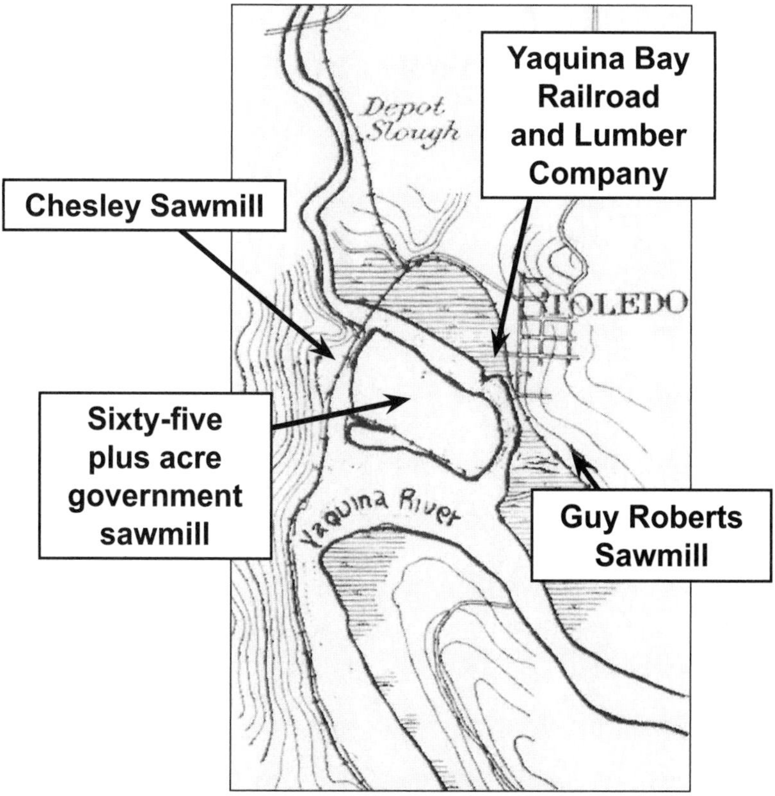

Figure B. 1918 Toledo sawmills and the 65-plus acre industrial area known as the "island."

Photograph courtesy of Lincoln County Historical Society, Newport, Oregon

4. Toledo waterfront, 1918. The soldier tent camp and the new spruce mill under construction lay beyond the storefronts and across Depot Slough on the "island."

Division.

While the government mill was under construction, the Yaquina Bay Railroad and Lumber Company (remembered in Toledo as the Fischer-Storey Sawmill) was manned by soldiers (Photograph 5). In early November 1918, the Army decided that soldiers working the sawmill would be more valuable elsewhere, and a crew of about twenty-five Japanese laborers was hired to work in their place.[19] This was the first time that a Japanese crew worked a sawmill in Lincoln County, and there is no indication that their arrival had any impact on the Toledo community.[20]

While locally, the new work crew made sure that the Toledo mill continued to produce, regionally, the overall shipments of airplane material from the Northwest amounted to one hundred forty three million board feet (mbf) in just fifteen months. Of this about forty-one mbf went to Great Britain, thirty-four mbf to France, fourteen mbf to Italy and fifty-two mbf (about thirty-six percent) stayed in the United States.[21] The total money invested in Oregon and Washington during this fifteen month period topped fifty-one million dollars (twenty three million dollars for purchases and twenty seven million dollars for operating costs).[22] In the end the United States paid twelve million dollars (about twenty-four percent) of the total invested in the Northwest.[23]

Photograph courtesy of Lincoln County Historical Society, Newport, Oregon

5. The Fir and Spruce Lumber Company, as pictured above in 1911, had changed its name briefly to the Yaquina Bay Railroad and Lumber Company in 1918.

Before the spruce mill could be completed, the war ended in November 1918. With the armistice, two important issues surfaced: sending the troops home and selling the assets in Oregon and Washington for salvage. As to the first concern, according to an article in the *Lincoln County Leader*, soldiers left as quickly as they had arrived:

> January tenth will see the last big train leave Yaquina with troops from south of Toledo... Toledo will see two squadrons leave very soon, possibly January 12th. When the other two squadrons will move is not known but the policy of getting the men in from the district as soon as

> possible will probably mean that the last squadrons will leave Toledo inside of a week or ten days.[24]

Six months later in July 1919, the government properties in Oregon and Washington were advertised for sale in the United States, Canada, Northern Europe and South America (Photograph 6). The goal was to recover at least ten cents for every dollar spent.[25] [About fourteen million dollars was eventually recovered.]

The Oregon properties remained unsold for a year before C.D. Johnson and other investors came forward with an acceptable offer to buy most of the government assets. Purchase negotiations started in July 1920. By September both parties reached an agreement.[26] The editor of the *Lincoln County Leader* clearly expressed the excitement in town, "This is the best news that has been received here in Toledo since the signing of the armistice. Everyone is wearing one of those smiles that won't come off. To say that we are all tickled to death is putting it mild."[27] The anticipated economic boon to Toledo was well received. By December 1920, the sale was complete and the newly-formed Pacific Spruce Corporation took possession of the assets in Lincoln County for a purchase price of two million dollars, payable in annual installments over a ten-year period. The newly purchased properties included the

6. This full page advertisement appeared in the July 17, 1919 Morning Oregonian.

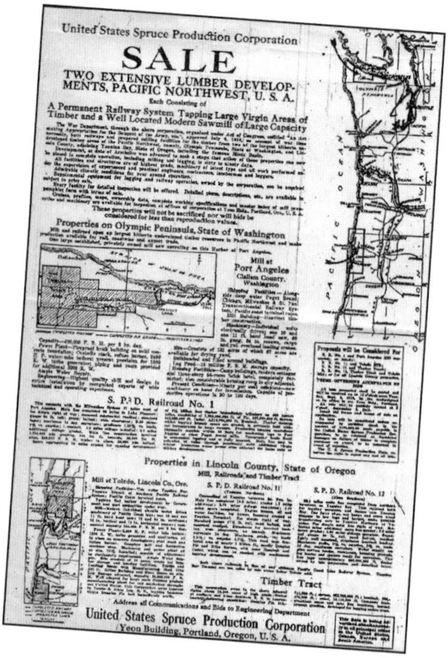

million dollar sawmill in Toledo, miscellaneous equipment, the Alsea Southern Railroad and a tract of land containing eight-hundred million board feet of timber.[28] Additionally, the log booms, or log holding areas, around the Toledo mill were filled with millions of board feet of logs ready for cutting.[29]

C.D. Johnson, a man with thirty-five years experience in the timber industry, was president of the new corporation. His office was located in downtown Portland, Oregon. His son C. Dean Johnson, II, was made vice-president and manager of the Toledo sawmill.[30]

Twelve months passed before the new corporation was ready to start work on its properties. Company officials made an announcement in December 1921 that in January a large force of men would begin work on the unfinished sawmill since there were a number of additions and improvements to be made before the mill could open for business. By the following February, over one hundred and forty men were on the company payroll,[31] with local men given hiring priority. Many of these early employees stayed with the mill for more than twenty years.

Table 1. Toledo Population Table.[32]

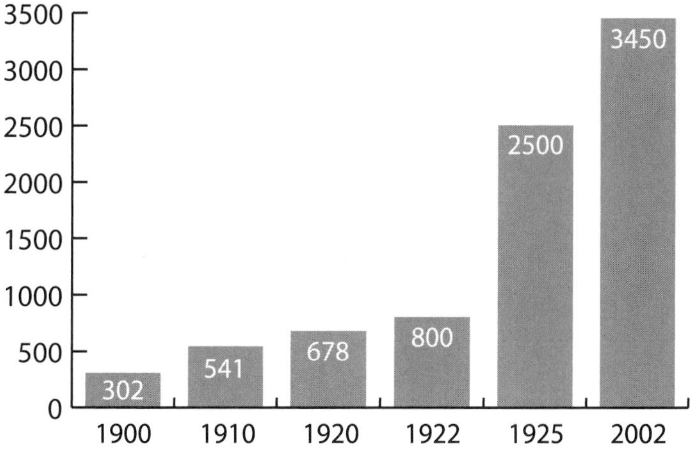

With the 1923 acquisition of a railroad going from Toledo north to Siletz, the Pacific Spruce Corporation had access to a tremendous amount of timber just a few miles north of Toledo. The Pacific Spruce sawmill was the largest old-growth sawmill in Oregon.[33]

In three years Toledo had tripled in size from eight hundred to twenty-five hundred people (Table 1). Never before, or since, has the town experienced such a three-year population explosion.

By 1925 the mill had the capacity to produce more than ten times the amount of lumber per day than any other mill in the county. Toledo was the busiest town in Lincoln County, claiming twenty percent of the county's population.[34] The impact of Pacific Spruce Corporation on Toledo and the county was tremendous. Eight hundred people lived in Toledo in 1922. By 1924 the Pacific Spruce Corporation payroll alone carried eight hundred employees (including men in the logging camps and the railroad shops).[35] The city of Toledo became the

Photograph courtesy of Lincoln County Historical Society, Newport, Oregon

7. Eastward view of the mill complex.[36]

1. *Baseball field*
2. *County Road*
3. *Japanese Housing*
4. *Original commercial Waterfront*
5. *Tokyo Slough*
6. *Depot Slough*
7. *Guy Roberts Sawmill*

center of industrial and agricultural activity in Lincoln County. Nearly every sector of the county did business in Toledo. For over forty years the big mill dominated the payroll and the panorama of the little town built on a hill (Photograph 7).

NOTES

[1]"Seek Light on Spruce in Lincoln," *Oregon Daily Journal*, 28 Aug. 1919.

[2]"Examiners See Mill at Toledo," *Oregon Daily Journal*, 31 Aug. 1919.

[3]"Seek Light," *Daily Journal*.

[4]There is a DeHaviland bi-plane on display at the Evergreen Aviation Museum, McMinnville, Oregon (503-434-4180).

[5]Gerald W. Williams, "The Spruce Production Division," *Forest History Today*, Spring 1999, 3.

[6]Williams, 3.

[7]Lloyd M. Palmer. *Steam Towards the Sunset* (Lincoln County Historical Society: Newport, Oregon, 2003), 29.

[8]Lloyd M. Palmer, telephone interview by author, December 6, 2004.

[9]"Fliers May Talk at Spruce Inquiry," *Morning Oregonian*, 26 Aug. 1919.

[10]State of Oregon Corporation Division Records. Salem, Oregon.

[11]"Load Car of Airplane Spruce," *Lincoln County Leader*, 8 March 1918.

[12]Palmer, *Steam Towards*, 38.

[13]"Heavy Freight Traffic on C.& E.," *Lincoln County Leader*, 2 Aug. 1918.

[14]"Toledo to Have Another Sawmill," *Lincoln County Leader*, 11 Jan. 1918.

[15]"Chesley Mill to Operate May 1st," *Lincoln County Leader*, 29 April 1918.

[16]"Government to Establish Cut-Up Mill," *Lincoln County Leader*, 10 May 1918.

[17]"Work Being Rushed on Government Mill," *Lincoln County Leader*, 2 Aug. 1918.

[18]"3000 Soldiers in Lincoln County," *Lincoln County Leader*, 12 July 1918.

[19]"Japanese Arrive to Work in Sawmill," *Lincoln County Leader*, 1 Nov. 1918.

[20]Japanese railroad section laborers worked for the Oregon Pacific Railroad in the 1890s out of Yaquina City located seven miles down river from Toledo. At the same time a Japanese garden located on the hill above Yaquina City supplied vegetables to Yaquina City and Newport. See Figure A page 3.

[21]"Spruce Investigation to be Ended Today," *Daily Home Journal*, 12 Sept. 1919.

[22]"Spruce Investigation," *Journal*.

[23]"Estimated Spruce Loss $35,796,322," *Morning Oregonian*, 13 Sept. 1919.

[24]"Troops Move Out of District Rapidly," *Lincoln County Leader*, 10 January 1919.

[25]"Estimated Spruce Loss," *Morning Oregonian*.

[26]"Government Spruce Holdings Sold," *Lincoln County Leader*, 3 Sept. 1919.

[27]"Government Spruce Holdings," *Leader*.

[28]Bolling Arthur Johnson, "Pacific Spruce Corporation & Subsidiaries", reprinted from the *Lumber World Review*, (1924): 13.

[29]"Examiners See," *Daily Journal*.

[30]Johnson, *Pacific Spruce*, 16.

[31]"Sawmill Notes," *Lincoln County Leader*, 3 Feb. 1922.

[32]Data compiled from different sources: 1900/1910/1920—*Lincoln County Leader*, 23 Aug. 1920. 1922—*Lincoln County Leader*, 18 Dec. 1921. 1925—*Lincoln County Leader,* 27 Aug. 1925. 2002—City of Toledo, City Hall records.

[33]"Pacific Spruce Corporation Purchases Entire Holdings Anderson & Middleton Including Railroad, Mill Site and Timber," *Lincoln County Leader*, 22 March 1923.

[34]Steve Wyatt, *The Bay Front Book* (Old Town Printers, Waldport, Oregon, 1999), 78.

[35]Johnson, *Pacific Spruce*, 13.

[36]The 1954 photograph shows the Georgia Pacific Mill, which was purchased in 1952 from the C.D. Johnson Lumber Company.

Chapter 3: Rumors Begin

1925 Pacific Spruce Corporation Plans to Hire Japanese Crew

In April 1925 after two years of operation, rumors spread throughout Toledo that the Pacific Spruce Corporation was going to hire Japanese resident labor to work on the "green-chain."[1] The green-chain was a process by which lumber was sorted into specific stacking pockets. Before the freshly cut boards were sent down the chain they were graded,[2] each piece marked with a black crayon indicating into which unit each board would be stacked. Along each side of the green-chain were approximately three hundred unit frames (stacking pockets), providing a sufficient number of spaces in which to slide and pile the lumber by grade, length, width, thickness and species of tree. Each unit was four feet wide with lumber piled about four feet high (Photograph 8). The work was back-breaking, and most mills had difficulty keeping reliable men at these stations. As mill management discussed ways to solve this problem, word got out that they were considering bringing in an outside labor force.

For the purpose of clarifying rumors in town about the mill's intentions, representatives of the Toledo Businessmen's League and Chamber of Commerce met with Pacific Spruce Corp. Vice-President, Dean Johnson, at his office Wednesday morning, April 29, 1925. Mr. Johnson informed the committee that he planned to bring in ten to twelve *Issei** workers the following month to do the jobs regular employees had not been performing well. He also told the representatives that his company had no thought of employing large

**For definition and pronounciation, see page xvi.*

Photograph courtesy of Lincoln County Historical Society, Newport, Oregon

8. 1923-Green-chain line. This sorting line was one of two five hundred foot long sorting areas. Both sorting areas had three moving chains.

numbers of Japanese and that he would be pleased to meet with the Chamber of Commerce and explain why the decision had been made. A discussion was scheduled for that Friday evening at eight o'clock.[3]

Before the scheduled meeting, Rosemary Schenck (Photograph 9), wife of Toledo City Marshal George Schenck, met privately with Dean Johnson to protest against bringing in Japanese labor.[4] She believed that the mill had agreed in 1922 not to hire "foreign labor" if the community provided private housing to accommodate the growing number of employees. To her way of thinking the people of Toledo had fulfilled their part of this "gentlemen's agreement." Unfortunately nothing in the research indicates how Dean Johnson responded during this meeting.

Friday evening arrived and the Chamber meeting room was

filled to capacity well before eight o'clock. Outside the building, a large crowd stood waiting impatiently. Chamber President, Mr. D. L. Peterson, decided to move the meeting to the street so that everyone could hear the proceedings. There were an estimated five hundred people in attendance.[5]

Photograph courtesy of Lincoln County Historical Society, Newport, Oregon

Rosemary Schenck
Lincoln County's Candidate
— for —
State Senator

9. November 3, 1932, campaign advertisement

Dean Johnson was the first person to speak. Expecting support from the community, he talked about his experience as a sawmill operator in various areas of the country. The local newspaper quotes Johnson as saying, "in all large plants there are certain kinds of labor that white men will not do satisfactorily. The American laborer has higher ambitions than accepting the lowest paid and hardest job on the works and stay with it."[6] He went on to say that the same situation was true in Toledo. He believed that the Japanese were the best workers to hire for this purpose. They had a reputation of being team players, which the green-chain often required. In addition, he knew that employing Japanese residents was good business since many of the orders for spruce came from Japan (where the lumber was used in the airplane industry).[7]

Rosemary Schenck spoke next and gave reasons for her objections to bringing in outside labor. She did not think that Pacific Spruce had any right to bring in the Japanese workers. Mrs. Schenck told the crowd that if the Japanese came to work, their presence would cause property values to go down, and she threatened extreme measures to prevent that from happening.[8] In her opinion, the "old-timers" and others had worked hard to develop the county and had not put forth their efforts intending that outsiders such as the Japanese should come in and reap the benefits. As Mrs. Schenck stated her case, a mill supporter in the crowd spoke out against her. The man said, "Why, you were just fish-eaters before the mill came to this town." Knowing the nutritional value of fish, Schenck pointed him out in the crowd and said, "Young man, if you had eaten more fish when you were younger, you would have more brains in your head today!"[9] Such a witty comeback was in keeping with her temperament.

In all fairness to Mrs. Schenck, there was some basis for her complaint. The two big issues from the town's point-of-view were property taxes and city water.

When Pacific Spruce Corporation purchased the Lincoln County properties in 1920, the federal government held onto the property title until the ten-year contract was paid in full. During this period, the property was taken off the tax rolls. Prior to 1918, these properties contributed about forty-five thousand dollars a year in county taxes. By not restoring the mill to the tax rolls, the loss of revenue placed a strain on county government as community leaders tried to construct and maintain roads, as well as other public works, without the valuable tax income from the Pacific Spruce Corporation.[10]

In regard to the water issue, Mrs. Schenck was upset at how some of the fresh water supplied by the city to Pacific Spruce Corporation was being used. The mill needed thousands of gallons of fresh water per day in order to run operations.[11] To meet the need, there was an agreement in place that the city would supply hundreds of thousands of gallons of water per day to the mill.[12] However, on the seventy-two acre industrial site were a number of homes, along with two large dormitories housing over eighty-two men and a large cafeteria.[13]

These buildings also received fresh water from the city for which the mill did not pay. Mrs. Schenck did not believe that these structures should be considered part of the original water agreement and should therefore pay a water use fee.[14]

Rosemary Schenck continued her list of complaints saying that Pacific Spruce was sawing logs in the Yaquina River and the resulting sawdust was destroying the salmon and oyster industry.

Although she did not discuss it at this meeting, Mrs. Schenck also felt that the Pacific Spruce Corp. had gotten two of their employees elected to the local school board to increase their influence in the community.[15] According to her, the two mill workers were put up for election against local candidates who had lived in the community all of their lives. Mill employees had been encouraged to vote in this election on company time, and those that went to vote received pay for their time away from work.

Mr. Frank W. Stevens, general manager of the mill, spoke next. He explained that the Japanese were not being brought in to replace current employees, but simply to meet an emergency. He insisted that there would be a small crew hired and that they would be segregated from the town, on mill property. "Not a single white man will lose his job. The Japs are not being brought in to take any one's place, but simply to meet an emergency."[16] Perhaps Stevens was suggesting that the local men working the two green-chain night shifts would be transferred to do other work at the mill. In addressing Mrs. Schencks' charge that Pacific Spruce was destroying the fish and oyster industries on the Yaquina River, he said that the Corporation had spent nearly fifteen thousand dollars to protect the fish and that a tile wall forty feet long had been built to catch all of the sawdust.

At the end of the meeting those present voted to adopt the following resolution:

> It is resolved, that we, the citizens of Toledo and vicinity, in mass meeting assembled, hereby protest and remonstrate against said proposed action of the Pacific Spruce Corporation in introducing and employing Japanese, Chinese, or any other foreign labor.[17]

The resolution triggered a series of events that culminated with the actions of a mob two-and-a-half months later.

From C.D. and Dean Johnsons' points of view the declaration had crossed over into private business decisions and meddled with company management. Ignoring the resolution—and the opinions expressed at the meeting—the Johnsons went forward with their plans to hire the Japanese.

When the Japanese Association in Portland became aware of the negative attitude expressed toward the Japanese in Toledo, they sent their Caucasian financial representative, Mr. John H. Velie, to investigate. He learned of the resolution issued May 1 and reported his findings back to Portland. Immediately the Japanese Employment Agency said that their office would not send men to work at the spruce mill in Toledo until antagonistic conditions had changed.[18]

On May 12 while C.D. Johnson was proceeding with his plans to hire outside labor, the Businessmen's League and Toledo Chamber of Commerce held a second meeting to clarify the May 1 declaration. A new and more restrictive resolution was passed barring specifically Japanese, Chinese, Negro, Hindu and other Oriental labor at the Pacific Spruce Mill.[19]

To counter this meddling in mill affairs, C.D. Johnson requested a Toledo Businessmen's League meeting be held June 26 at the Pacific Spruce Cafeteria (photographs 10 and 11). He wanted to discuss rethinking the issue. Prior to the June 26 meeting, at Johnson's urging, Mr. W. G. Ide, manager of the State Chamber of Commerce, visited Toledo and spoke to local businessmen on the importance of cooperation

Photograph and photocopy courtesy of Harland Pratt, Corvallis, Oregon

CAFETERIA

10. 1923–A group of men waiting for dinner at the Pacific Spruce Cafeteria.[20]

PACIFIC SPRUCE CAFETERIA
Best Eating Place in Toledo
(AND THEN SOME)
EXCELLENT FOOD AND SERVICE AT MODERATE PRICES

11. An advertisement in the 1924 Toledo Telephone Directory.

between the mill and the town. In addition, Mr. Velie talked to businessmen about the advantages of hiring Japanese labor.[21] The June 26 meeting was closed to the public.

C.D. Johnson came from his Portland office to attend. He gave a lengthy talk regarding company efforts to run the green-chain successfully with local labor and explained that those efforts had failed, frequently delaying operations. Johnson felt that the corporation had a right to solve its own problems in its own way without community interference. To solve the problem he would bring in a sufficient number of Japanese, about sixty men, to work two shifts on the night green-chain.[22]

Photograph by Ted W. Cox—2004

12. C. Dean Johnson, III, standing by a picture of his father Dean Johnson. September 30, 2004.

Dean Johnson spoke next emphasizing his father's frustrations. He stated that the green-chain lumber was often poorly sorted, making it necessary to handle the boards a second time, resulting in a slowdown of overall operations. He pointed out that the mill could not economically operate on a six-day workweek with the current inefficient green-chain performance.[23]

C.D. Johnson's grandson, C. Dean Johnson, III, was a year old in 1925. During a 2004 interview at his home near Portland (Photograph 12) he shared some insights into both his grandfather's and his father's decision to hire a Japanese crew:

> The green-chain pullers were mostly Scandinavian. They were always big, tough guys, very proud and able men. They came with a pair of gloves with gauntlets, had a leather apron and made it quite clear that they were up to the job. The problem with them was that they were also very independent. One guy would have several pockets [areas four feet wide to stack specific lumber into] (Photograph 8) for which he would be assigned to pull a certain grade of lumber off of the green-chain. When the mill was cutting, the wood would sometimes come out in globs and at times it was overwhelming for one man. The guy next to him never offered a bit of help. Besides, they would not ask for help and they would not accept it. It was a matter of great pride.
>
> The Japanese had a different attitude. They were short guys, fairly muscular but not nearly as tough as the Scandinavians. They worked as a team and would pack and stack up the lumber for the next guy following them. They could pull off three or four pieces at once instead of one at a time, and were able to do more than the Swedes by a significant amount.
>
> The Japanese were brought in to see if they could help get things done better. Dad thought they would do things more efficiently. It was not a matter of wages but who could do the job better.
>
> The people in town who protested had no connection with the mill and had very little understanding of why the Japanese were there.[24]

Mr. Johnson emphasized that the decision to hire *Issei* labor was strictly an operational assessment: a more efficient green-chain labor force meant a more efficient operation of the mill overall.

Mr. John Velie made another trip from Portland to speak at the June 26 meeting. He emphasized that the country of Japan was buying more than sixty percent of the lumber manufactured in the Pacific Northwest suggesting that the hiring of Japanese employees made good business sense.

The meeting had been organized to convince the businessmen of Toledo to reverse their resolutions of May 1 and 12. At the end of the meeting, Frank Stevens introduced a new resolution to do just that by asking the businessmen to rescind the previous two resolutions. Johnson insisted that the vote be taken by roll call, the representatives of each business house answering "yes" or "no" as their names were called. The result was forty-five to eleven in favor of rescinding the previous resolutions. Furthermore, the businessmen agreed not to interfere with the corporation's labor policy in the future.[25] As this information reached the Japanese Association in Portland, preparations began to bring the first of two *Issei* crews to Toledo.

While the June 26 meeting was taking place in the Pacific Spruce Cafeteria, a separate rally was held on Hill Street [today known as Main Street] by those who outwardly opposed hiring Japanese labor. The open rally was attended by community leaders not invited to the businessmen's meeting, as well as J. O. Young of the State Federation of Labor and anyone else interested. Those gathered to hear speeches that evening reaffirmed the resolution adopted May 12 against the Japanese workforce. During the rally, the group decided to form a permanent local organization at their next meeting to be held the following Tuesday, June 30. They also asked that their supporters immediately begin boycotting all of the merchants who had voted to rescind the resolution.[26]

As planned, the protesters met at the ball park on June 30. Between two hundred and three hundred people were present. They voted to form an organization called "The Lincoln County Protective League" (LCPL). Officers of the LCPL were selected as follows: W. A. Lindsay, President; Verne Ross and E. H. Dunham, Vice Presidents; Mrs. Rosemary Schenck, Mrs. Ethel Bateman and Gordon Ferris, Secretaries; Mrs. Alice Waugh, Mrs. R. A. Anderson, Fred Chambers, Miss Lillian Tindall, R. A. (Harry T.) Pritchard and W. R. Stokes, Board of Directors. The League's purpose: "To use all honorable means to protect our communities from the employment of Japanese or other Oriental labor."[27] During the previous weekend, they had circulated petitions and obtained hundreds of signatures supporting their cause.

On Wednesday, July 8, Rosemary Schenck delivered copies of the LCPL petition to Governor Walter M. Pierce in Salem and to the Japanese Consul in Portland, Hisakichi Okamoto. Consul Okamoto informed Mrs. Schenck that monitoring employment of Japanese nationals was not part of his duties.[28]

While in Portland Mrs. Schenck gave an interview to the *Morning Oregonian* in which she said, "There is bound to be trouble if the Japanese are brought into Toledo, and we want the Governor to have facts of the situation at hand in that event."[29] She was determined to keep the *Issei* out of Toledo.

With the threat of retaliation hanging over their heads, the Pacific Spruce Corporation proceeded with their plan to bring in Japanese labor to work the green-chain.

NOTES

[1]"Pacific Spruce to Employ Japanese for Heavy Manual Labor," *Lincoln County Leader,* 30 April 1925.

[2]"Case L9709," National Archives-Pacific AK Region, Seattle, Washington.

[3]"Pacific Spruce to Employ Japanese," *Leader.*

[4]"Big Mass Meeting Adopts Resolution Opposing Jap Labor," *Lincoln County Leader,* 7 May 1925.

[5]"Big Mass Meeting," *Leader.*

[6]"Big Mass Meeting," *Leader.*

[7]"Japanese Rumpus at Toledo Probed," *Oregon Statesman*, 14 July 1925.

[8]"Big Mass Meeting," *Leader.*

[9] Earl Roberts, interview by author, written notes, Toledo, Oregon, June 4, 2004.

[10]"McCammant-Johnson Scrap Airs Condition in Lincoln County," *Lincoln County Leader,* 28 Jan 1926.

[11]Fresh water availability was vital for the mill to operate. Although three rivers surround Toledo, they all contain a percentage of saltwater brought in by the ocean tide. Up to 400,000 gallons of fresh water per day was supplied to the Pacific Spruce mill from the City reservoir, which was located a few miles away. *Lincoln County Leader*, 28 Jan. 1926.

[12]"Dr. Burgess Says Council Should Collect Water Rentals," *Lincoln County Leader,* 30 April 1925.

[13]Bolling Arthur Johnson, "Pacific Spruce Corporation & Subsidiaries", reprinted from the *Lumber World Review,* (1924): 59, 65. In 1922 Pacific Spruce Corporation purchased seven acres of reclaimed tideland adjoining their property and built housing for their employees.

[14]"Dr. Burgess Says Council," *Leader.*

[15]"Japanese Rumpus at Toledo," *Leader.*

[16]"Big Mass Meeting," *Leader.*

[17]"Big Mass Meeting," *Leader.*

[18]"Toledo Japanese Deportation," *Oregon Voter*, 12 Sept. 1925.

[19]"Businessmen of Toledo Oppose the Japs," *Lincoln County Leader*, 14 May, 1925.

[20]Johnson, *Lumber World Review*, 82.

[21]"Toledo Businessmen Rescind Action Against Orientals," *Lincoln County Leader*, 2 July 1925.

[22]"Toledo Scene of Riot," *Yaquina Bay News,* 16, July 1925.

[23]"Toledo Businessmen Rescind Action Against Orientals," *Lincoln County Leader,* 2 July 1925.

[24]C.D. Johnson III, telephone interview by author, 1 Oct. 2004.

[25]"Toledo Businessmen Rescind," *Leader.*

[26]"Employee of Pacific Spruce Corporation Condemns 'Agitators," *Lincoln County Leader,* 23 July 1925.

[27]"Mass Meeting Friday Reaffirms Resolutions Against Orientals," *Lincoln County Leader,* 2 July 1925.

[28]"Japanese Labor Target," *Morning Oregonian,* 9 July 1925.

[29]"Japanese Labor Target," *Oregonian.*

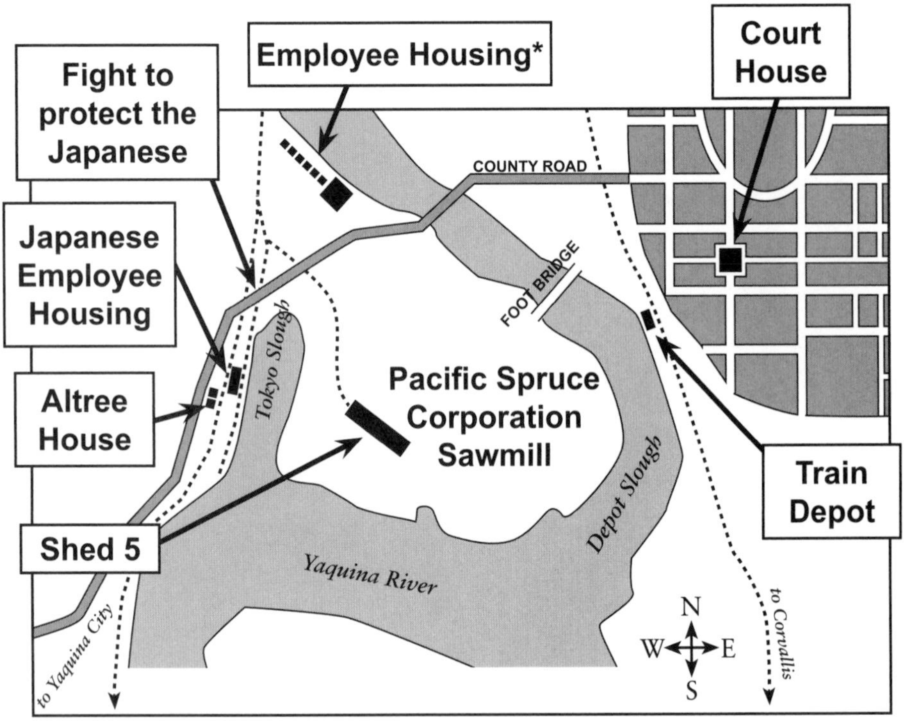

Figure C. 1925–Layout of the Pacific Spruce Sawmill and surrounding area.

* This employee housing was constructed on seven acres of land purchased in 1922 making a total of seventy-two acres of mill property.

Chapter 4:
The Confrontation

1925 Three Days That Made History In Toledo, Oregon

On Friday July 10, 1925, the daily passenger train from Corvallis, Southern Pacific #401, pulled into the Toledo Depot at 4:20 p.m. (Photograph 13).[1] Pacific Spruce mill officials were waiting at the depot. Twenty-seven Japanese (two with families), four Filipino and one Korean gentleman (all contract workers) disembarked and were immediately driven to a group of sixteen duplex houses located on company property about a half-mile away. The mill had a private railroad spur that ran between the houses and the slough.

Photograph courtesy of Lincoln County Historical Society, Newport, Oregon

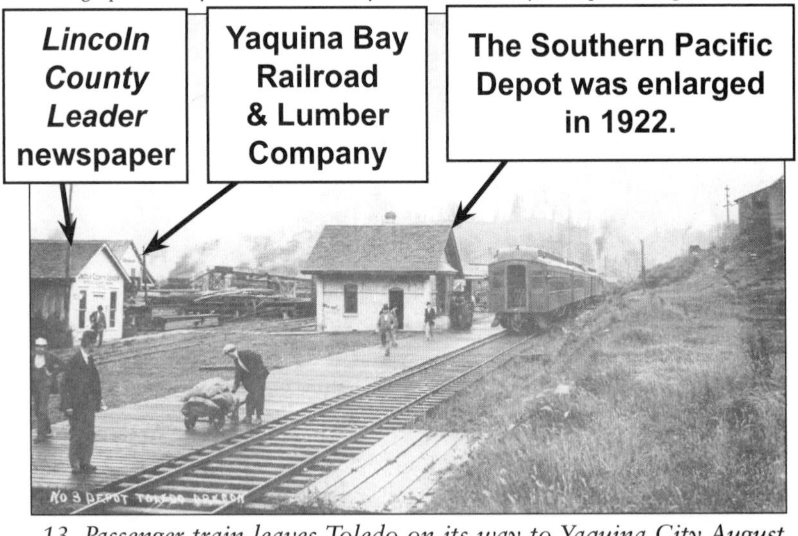

13. Passenger train leaves Toledo on its way to Yaquina City August 27, 1918. Background buildings include the Lincoln County Leader *on the left and Yaquina Bay Railroad and Lumber Company.*

The housing had been built the previous month on the edge of what would soon be called Tokyo Slough (Photograph 14).[2] Each house had indoor plumbing and electricity. The kitchens and bathrooms were supplied with hot and cold running water. Although the bathroom had a bathtub and washbasin, there was no toilet. On the west side of the housing, next to the railroad track, a communal outhouse was provided with multiple holes that dropped directly into the slough. The communal outhouse serviced all of the homes within the housing complex. The

Photograph courtesy of Lincoln County Historical Society, Newport, Oregon

14. This 1925 picture shows the construction of the Japanese housing complex in the center foreground of the photograph.

Photograph courtesy of Valley Library, Oregon State University, Corvallis, Oregon

15. Tamakichi Ogura is standing on the left. Ichiro Kawamoto, foreman, is standing on the right. Photograph was taken in July 1926 in Portland, Oregon.

foreman's house was separated from the duplex housing by just a few yards.[3]

Lifetime Toledo resident Harry Hawkins was a child when these homes were constructed. In an interview he described the buildings, "They were nice little cottages. There must have been 20 of them. I remember playing in those houses when I was a kid."[4] Well constructed, these houses were inexpensive, serviceable homes.

The Tokyo Slough complex was built to house about sixty people. On another area of the seventy-plus acre industrial complex were other homes and two rooming buildings that could accommodate over one hundred workers. Employees living in the company housing on mill property could go to and from their jobs without coming into contact with the local population.

Ichiro Kawamoto (Photograph 15) contracted with the Pacific Spruce Corporation to supply sixty (mostly *Issei*) workers. He had immigrated to the United States in 1900 and had been a resident of Oregon since about 1907. Prior to his contract with Pacific Spruce Corporation he worked as manager of a hop yard in the Willamette Valley. Kawamoto left that position when he was offered employment with the Pacific Spruce Corporation as crew foreman for five dollars per day.[5] He was accompanied by his wife, Ito, and their three children (son Kiyoshi, daughter Shizue and son George).[6] Mrs.

Ito Kawamoto was hired to cook for the Asian crew at a wage of three dollars a day.[7]

Tamakichi Ogura (Photograph 15) left his farm job in Multnomah County to work the green-chain for four dollars and fifty cents a day. Mr. Koichi Yamano was another *Issei* employed by Kawamoto. Mr. Yamano brought his wife, Kazu, who was hired to prepare meals along with Mrs. Kawamoto.[8]

On Saturday, Mrs. Kawamoto and others walked to downtown Toledo. City Marshal (Chief of Police)[9] George Schenck (Photograph 16) confronted them. He ordered Mrs. Kawamoto and her Japanese companions to go back to their houses and to leave town by the next day. According to her, he said that they would be thrown out and killed if they did not leave. Schenck later denied Mrs. Kawamoto's allegations:

> The charge that I threatened to kill or in any way harm any of the Japanese who were deported from Toledo some time ago is a falsehood. I warned the fellows to stay off the street for their own safety.[10]

Photograph courtesy of Valley Library, Oregon State University, Corvallis, Oregon

16. George Schenck was a member of the Toledo Police Force for seventeen years. Photograph was taken July 1926 in Portland, Oregon.

Being an outsider in a new and unfamiliar town, Mrs. Kawamoto may have felt more threatened than Schenck intended, intimidated by Schenck's police authority.

The same morning that Mrs. Kawamoto and her companions were told to leave downtown Toledo, an unknown person posted handbills, printed on red paper, announcing that a rally would be held at the city baseball field at six o'clock that evening in order to decide what actions would be taken the following day to confront the Japanese workers.[11] The handbills were printed in the *Lincoln County Leader* newspaper office that morning:

> Mass meeting by the citizens of Lincoln County at the Toledo ballpark, 6 p.m., July 11. Purpose to decide the question now and forever as to whether we want our citizens replaced by Japanese, or other foreign labor by the Pacific Spruce Mill or other industries in this county. The Japs are here now. A Taxpayer.[12]

Organizers hoped for a large turnout at the gathering that evening, believing that the anti-Japanese sentiment was predominant in the community and that people only needed a leader to bring them to action. Reflecting on the mood of the town, clothing store owner Harry Pritchard believed that the presence of the Japanese was opposed because of fear that they would replace local labor in the mill.[13]

The Toledo ballpark (Photograph 17) had been used over the years for various public meetings, such as advertised in the handbill above, and as seen in a 1924 assembly (Photograph 18). Although the gathering in the 1924 photograph is one with hundreds in attendance, the anti-Japanese rally announced by the handbill for July 11, 1925, was sparsely attended with only seventy people coming to hear the speeches.

Photograph by Ted W. Cox—2004

17. The Toledo Baseball Field as it looked in 2004.

Many thought nothing serious would result from this meeting since the gathering attracted so few people.[14]

Mr. H. T. Pritchard was the first to speak at the assembly. He told the crowd that he did not want Japanese in Toledo community life because they would be taking jobs away from local families. His suggestion for the following day was to confront the Japanese foreman and inform him that his crew was not wanted in Toledo.[15]

Pritchard also told those attending the rally that residents who had pioneered in the area were hoping for a brighter economic future through employment opportunities with the Pacific Spruce Corporation. This new source of income would offset their poor revenues from ranching. He recognized that the Japanese themselves were not at fault for seeking employment where they could find it.[16]

William Colvin spoke next. He went beyond Pritchard's suggestion of simply telling the Japanese that they weren't wanted to urging people to physically throw out the Japanese. "Now is time to act," Colvin shouted out.[17] He also argued that property values would go down if the Japanese were allowed to stay, that this was a serious situation, and some action should be taken, "The Japs already are here and there will be more."[18] Colvin's intemperance further fed the volatile

Photograph courtesy of Lincoln County Historical Society, Newport, Oregon

18. 1924–Public Meeting at the Toledo Baseball Field

situation.

Mr. J. M. Kimmel, an accountant at the mill, went to the meeting on behalf of mill management. Another mill employee, Mr. J. H. Inskeep, also attended the meeting. Both men recall Colvin getting the crowd stirred up with fiery rhetoric.

Rosemary Schenck was the third speaker. Like Colvin, she indicated that the time for talking was past, "Everything women can do has been done," she said. "Now it's time for red-blooded men to do as they did with the Japs at Longview."[19] Mrs. Schenck warned that if the situation was not resolved by the following day (Sunday) she feared the Pacific Spruce Corp. would ask for state militia to be sent in on Monday to protect the Japanese workers.[20] She urged everyone to show up on the waterfront the next day at two in the afternoon.[21]

As Sunday morning dawned, the buzz and clatter of industrial activity was silent. William Keyes wrote the following lead to an editorial in the *Lincoln County Leader* two weeks after the incident:

> July 12 was a beautiful day in Toledo. The surrounding hills seemed peaceful and quiet. You could see people scattered along Toledo's main street in small groups discussing the coming event, which was to take place at two o'clock that afternoon. There had been trouble brewing among the people for weeks, and now it was coming to head.[22]

Although there is no way of knowing, one can't help but wonder if any of these scattered groups anticipated how the unfolding events would later impact their small community. By mid-morning, cars displaying banners drove around Toledo and Newport, drawing attention to the two o'clock assembly at the Toledo waterfront.[23]

Not everyone was in favor of confronting the Japanese. Arguments over the issue were heated and practically everyone in town took a position on one side or the other. There were many people who did not want a confrontation with the mill or the Japanese work crew, including business owners pressured by mill leaders to stay out of mill management decisions.

Harry Hawkins was five-years-old when the Japanese came to Toledo (Photograph 19). In an interview with Connie Guardino he recalled how his family avoided the whole situation by leaving town that Sunday morning:

> I remember a picnic at Siletz with a whole lot of people who didn't want to get involved! It was a Sunday and my Dad and uncle knew problems were brewing with the imported Japanese laborers at the . . . lumber mill. [My family] wanted no part of it. When we came back from the picnic, it was all over with...
>
> I know some of the people involved got sued and a good portion of their lives were spent paying for damages done to the Japs who were railroaded out of town . . .[24]

Although children of Harry's age had no way of understanding the significance of the mob's actions, businessmen who had promised corporate officers they would not interfere with the mill's business decisions removed themselves and their families from the upcoming demonstration.

Mr. G. W. Hall, editor of the *Lincoln County Leader*, did not attend the two o'clock rally, although he had attended and written articles on all of the previous related gatherings. He later said he didn't go to the waterfront because he was afraid it might turn into mob violence.[25]

Photograph courtesy of Patricia Sturdevant Dye, Family Collection

19. 1927 – Harry Hawkins in the Second Grade

Although the Lincoln County Protective League had been working in an orderly manner up to this point, the mounting tension spilled into a flare-up that Sunday morning. Mamie Altree (Photograph 20) was working in her family garden just a few yards up the hillside from the Japanese housing when she saw two men on the Southern Pacific railroad right-of-way just below her. As they approached the Japanese compound, she heard them yelling and saw Mr. Kawamoto, the Japanese foreman, come out of his house to confront them. When asked what she had heard she replied, "What was said was profane,"[26] adding that the two men made threats of killing and hanging the Japanese.

Photograph courtesy of Lincoln County Historical Society, Newport, Oregon

20. Photograph of Mamie Altree as she appeared in the 1910s.

Tamakichi Ogura also witnessed this incident. He described what he saw:

> Two men came near the Japanese camp first. They said to get the women and children away at once.
>
> "What for?" We asked.
>
> "Great things are to happen this afternoon," they said.[27]

Based on Ogura's description above, the *Issei* workers had reason to fear some of the people in town.

When two o'clock arrived about fifty men and two hundred women and children gathered at the port dock in front of William S. Colvin's general merchandise store as planned.[28]

Before starting their march, the group listened to Colvin and Pritchard deliver speeches of protest.

Arthur B. Griswald recalled Colvin urging the demonstrators to action. Colvin argued that the Pacific Spruce Corporation brought the Japanese workers into Toledo, and it was now up to the citizenry of the town to kick the Japanese out whether peacefully or by force. With his skewed version of nationalism he said, "I appeal to every man who respects his flag to join the line."[29] Colvin asked for a volunteer from the American Legion to carry the American flag from his store. When no one came forward, he handed the flag to an intoxicated Martin H. Germer who walked in front of the crowd as a flag bearer.[30] As the column organized, children jostled for their place in line.[31]

Colvin, Charles A. Buck, H. T. Pritchard, Frank Sturdevant, and L. D. Emerson were among those leading the column of protesters along the boardwalk.[32] The crowd followed the railroad tracks to the county road, passing by the baseball field.

Owen Hart, his brother, Rollie, and Chris Bredstead had gone to play in a Sunday baseball game but found that the game had been cancelled. They were at the ball field when the protesters passed by. Owen and Chris got caught up in the excitement and joined in.[33]

The crowd then crossed over the bridge at Depot Slough (Photographs 21 and 22). The whole course had taken fifteen to twenty minutes to walk. At the overpass a private planked road forked off onto mill property and went alongside Tokyo Slough to the Japanese housing about fifty yards away.

C.D. Johnson, Dean Johnson and a group of deputized Pacific Spruce employees were standing on the platform piling separating the public easement from private mill property and stopped the group from going any further. The Johnsons, who had been deputized the day before by Sheriff George Horsfall,

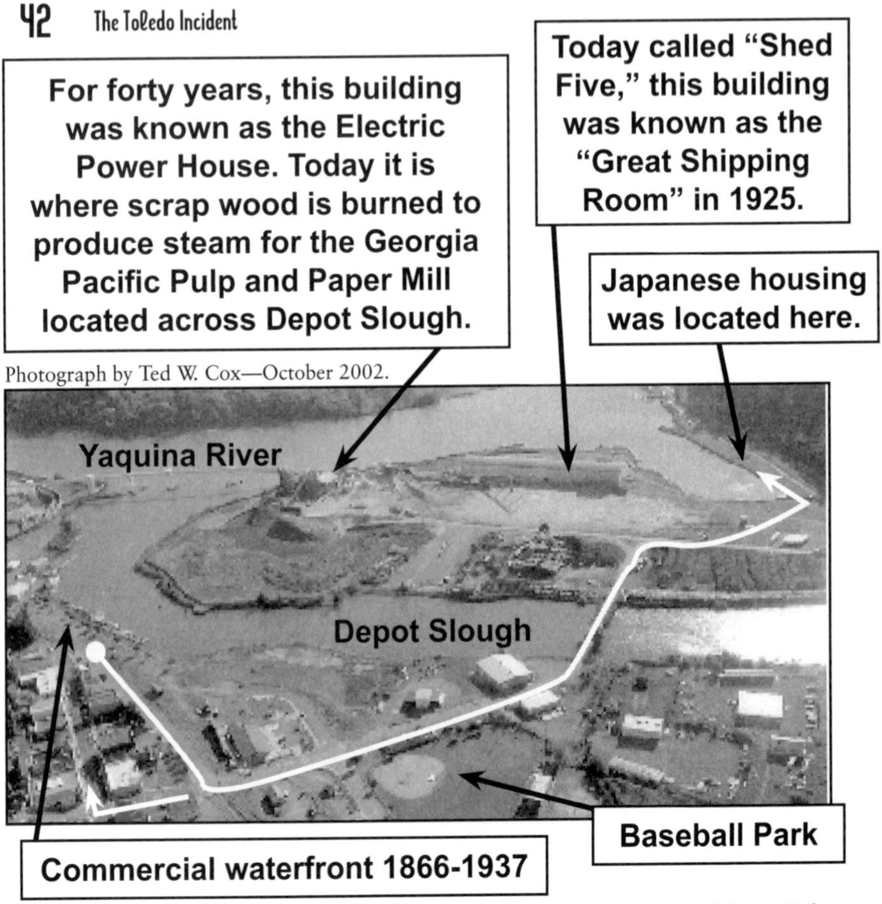
For forty years, this building was known as the Electric Power House. Today it is where scrap wood is burned to produce steam for the Georgia Pacific Pulp and Paper Mill located across Depot Slough.
Today called "Shed Five," this building was known as the "Great Shipping Room" in 1925.
Japanese housing was located here.
Yaquina River
Depot Slough
Baseball Park
Commercial waterfront 1866-1937

Photograph by Ted W. Cox—October 2002.

21. 2002–aerial view. The white arrows indicate the route to and from Tokyo Slough taken by the mob on July 12, 1926.

were determined to protect their property and their right to manage their company as they best determined.

Pritchard, acting as spokesman for the demonstrators, approached C.D. Johnson (Photographs 23 and 24) and asked if he could see the "head man" (referring to Japanese foreman Ichiro Kawamoto). Almost immediately Johnson pushed Pritchard in the chest and told him to get off the property.[34] The protesters who had held back up to this point started moving closer. Aware of the emotionally charged air, Johnson promptly drew a line indicating a point of trespass. He warned the crowd not to cross the line and said, "Your apparent inten-

Photograph by Ted W. Cox—2004

22. Tokyo Slough in 2004. Shed Five located middle right above is used today (2004) for storage and railroad car wood chip dumping.

tions are foolish."[35] As the throng moved closer an old lady with a stick was about to hit Johnson in the face, and men beyond the Southern Pacific right-of-way began picking up rocks. The group of indignant protesters had quickly turned into an angry mob.

Most of the women and children went onto the county road overpass to get a good view of the action, which also kept them off the company property as C.D. Johnson had warned. Many of these people were yelling and urging the fifty-plus men to move on.[36] "Down with the Japs," "Out With the Japs" and "Hang the Japs" were repeated over and over.[37]

Sheriff Horsfall had deputized mill office manager John F. Markham the night before. At the moment Johnson was threatened by the old lady with the stick, Markham, who was standing near Johnson, drew his handgun and warned the crowd, "Gentlemen, I represent the law, stand back." He pointed the gun into the crowd at close range, "Stop or

Photographs courtesy of Lincoln County Historical Society, Newport, Oregon

23. C.D. Johnson in 1923. He was deputized the day before the 1925 riot.

24. Dean Johnson in 1923. He was deputized the day before the 1925 riot.

I'll have to kill somebody. I'm a deputy sheriff, and it's my duty I'm doing."[38] C.D. Johnson then pointed his finger at Markham as he said to Pritchard, "If he shoots a half-dozen of you, you're to blame." Pritchard replied to Johnson, "There are no guns in our crowd," and made no effort to leave.[39]

As long as Markham had the gun in his hand, the mob was kept at bay. Suddenly, fifteen year-old Sonny Carson attacked Markham. The youth's hands shot up, pulling the revolver out of Markham's hand and the riot started.[40] Markham swung at a member of the mob but was quickly overwhelmed and severely beaten.

During the fight Owen Hart (Photograph 25) was hit in the face and knocked momentarily unconscious. He also lost two teeth during the clash.[41]

Another company deputy, Frank W. Stevens (Photograph 26), put his hands up in an attempt to stop the surging mob and was told, "We don't want anything but the Japs. We're here to get them and we're going to do it."[42] Overwhelmed by their numbers, Stevens couldn't stop the horde from pushing past him as Martin Germer carried the flag onto the platform where Stevens had been standing just moments before.

People were yelling, "Get the Japs, string them up." Company Deputy George C. Allen noticed the smell of alcohol in the air as he did his best to get control of the situation. He was quickly overrun as someone said, "get out of the way."[43] Allen was then pushed to the ground. Pritchard courteously picked up Allen's hat and handed it to him then continued towards the Japanese housing.[44] As the rioters passed them, C.D. Johnson and his defeated men followed.

Photograph courtesy of Patricia Sturdevant Dye Family Collection

25. Owen Hart, circa 1928.

Ichiro and Ito Kawamoto had been watching from their house as the fight described above broke out. They were alarmed with the unfolding drama and retreated into their home, locking the door in hope of protecting themselves and their children.[45] They heard rocks and sticks hitting the houses as the mob rushed in.[46]

A.R. Richardson, a sixty-year-old contractor, had picked up Markham's handgun during the fight at the property line. He now carried the pistol close to

Photograph courtesy of Lincoln County Historical Society, Newport, Oregon

26. Frank W. Stevens in 1923. He was deputized the night before the 1925 riot.

his body as he walked towards the Japanese houses. He might have been protecting the gun from the rest of the crowd, but the fact that it was loaded made the potential for deadly force very real.[47]

As with the threats she'd witnessed earlier that day from her backyard garden, Mamie Altree now saw the noisy mob throwing rocks and sticks into the compound as they approached. She saw Germer carrying the American flag and recognized Owen Hart who was in pain from his injuries and now looking for the man who hit him. She heard people yelling, "Bring them out, bring out the Japs" repeatedly. She also saw A.R. Richardson carrying the gun. Mrs. James Burns of Eddyville was also present when the mob entered the Japanese housing. As with Altree's observations, Mrs. Burns later described similar events.[48]

When the fifty-plus rioters entered the housing area, they immediately scattered among the four or five alleys that ran between the homes (Photograph 27). With the women and children watching from the railroad overpass, there still remained twice as many men (and a few women) in the mob as there were Japanese.[49]

Owen Hart entered the housing area with Chris Bredstead looking for the man who had knocked out his teeth. He thought it was Bob Richardson and was about to hit him when someone told him that it was not Richardson but a guy named Lyall R. Bolton. Hart "started looking for Bolton and when [he] found him among the Japanese houses, Hart offered to finish the fight."[50] The two men resolved their dispute then parted.

As the mob attempted to get at the Japanese, Hart, in the frenzy and chaos of the riot, crawled through an unlocked window to get inside one of the houses.[51] Meeting no resistance he unlocked the door and told the frightened inhabitants to go outside. At the same time Germer was outside rushing

Photograph courtesy of Lincoln County Historical Society, Newport, Oregon

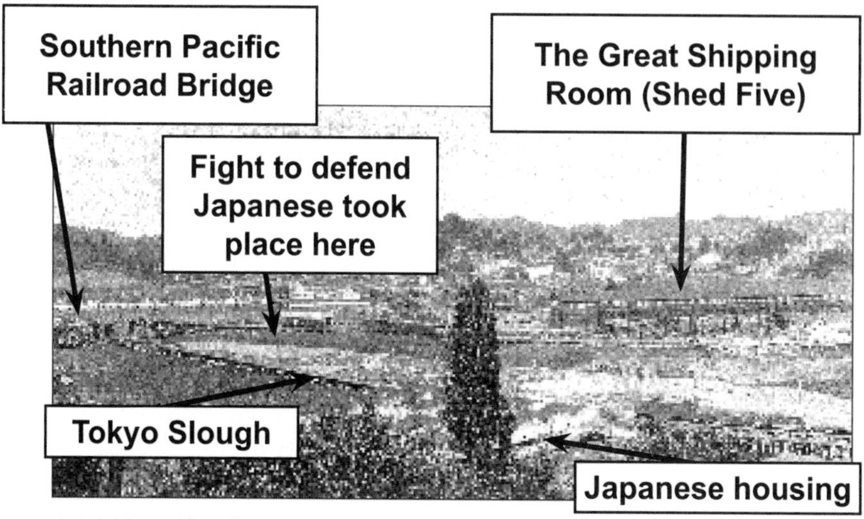

27. Tokyo Slough in 1926. The Japanese housing is located in the center foreground of the picture.

wildly about, waving the flag and urging the mob to "get them out!"[52] All of the Japanese were ordered to pack their bags and wait outside.

One of the mob members knocked on the door of Filipino Donato Angillis and asked him to come outside. The man asked Angillis if he was Japanese and he answered, "no." The trespasser then made it clear to Angillis that none of the Asians were welcome in town and that an automobile was being provided for his departure. The intruder then moved on to another house.[53]

At the foreman's house, Mrs. Kawamoto looked on in fright as William S. Colvin and two other men broke into her home using a big piece of wood as a battering ram.[54] They told Mr. Kawamoto to get out of the house in "two minutes." He asked why and they replied, "It don't make any difference why, we don't allow Japs around here any more." Kawamoto resisted, saying, "I belong with the mill and am going to stay right here." With that act of defiance one of the men said, "If you don't get out I'll hang you up and kill you.[55] Kawamoto repeated that he was not going anywhere. Two of the men grabbed him and threw him down on the floor and for a second time demanded he leave:

> I was hurt and couldn't get up. I couldn't say anything I was too scared. Then they kicked me, pulled me up and socked my jaw. My nose began to bleed. Still I didn't . . . go and the fellows took me by the arms and led me out. I was so scared I could hardly talk. My wife and babies were crying.[56]

While testifying about this episode, Mrs. Kawamoto said, "They kicked his face and he bled much. I thought he was cut with a knife." She said that two white men pushed her husband out of the house, and she followed holding her baby, George, along with her other two children (three-and-a-half year old Kiyoshi and two-year old Shizue). She said, "I felt very sorry, I never felt such a feeling in my life."[57] Mrs. Kawamoto explained, "I thought my husband and my children and I would be killed."[58] She stood by the house as her husband was taken towards the duplex housing.

Kawamoto tried to reason with Colvin on behalf of the *Issei*. He told Colvin if the people of Toledo were so determined to make the Japanese leave, then at least let them wait until the next day when a scheduled train would be available for departure (#402 at 12:55 a.m.).[59] Colvin would not agree and Kawamoto had to give in. He said, "we go" and began knocking on doors to encourage his crew to pack up and come out of their houses. Peter Tangen, one of the mob members commented later that Kawamoto went to at least three of the houses telling his workers to come out.[60] While Ichiro was separated from his wife and trying to organize the other Japanese employees he saw Sheriff Horsfall arrive along with Deputy Jess Daniel and Deputy Plank.[61] When the Sheriff arrived the Japanese were not putting up any resistance. Out of fear of further harm to himself, Ichiro did not talk to the Sheriff. He was concerned for his life and the lives of his wife and children.

Horsfall and Daniels ordered the mob to leave as an intoxicated Martin Germer resisted the Sheriff. Germer was immediately arrested for trespassing, along with William Colvin whom Sheriff Horsfall had noticed leaving Kawamoto's house. Deputy Daniels took the two men towards the jailhouse while Horsfall began writing down names of the fifty-plus people present.

Nothing in the research indicates that Sheriff Horsfall questioned anyone about Markham's handgun (Photograph 28). A.R. Richardson had probably thrown the pistol into Tokyo Slough by this time.

Photograph by Ted W. Cox—2004, courtesy of Lincoln County Historical Society, Newport, Oregon.

28. Deputy Markham's handgun that was dredged from Tokyo Slough.

The crowd was starting to break up when Germer and Colvin returned, yelling, "Come on fellows, the Japs haven't gone yet. They've got to get out this afternoon." When the mayhem rekindled, Germer again rushed wildly about, waving the flag and yelling, "Get them out! Get them out!"[62] Archie L. McMurray said at the trial that by the time Germer returned, most of the Japanese were already huddled outside of their houses.[63]

When C.D. Johnson saw Colvin and Germer return he approached Sheriff Horsfall and said in frustration, "Sheriff, I turn the property over to you." Then he left with his men and walked to the company office building located across the slough. From there they watched the outcome, which took about another forty-five minutes.[64]

Tamakichi Ogura later recalled, "They were pulling my shoulder and everywhere was a great noise, and I was falling down." The people in the mob told him that he was not wanted. During this chaos Ogura approached Deputy Daniels for help. Daniels said, "You better get out of this town or they're going to kill you!"[65] Ogura replied, "Everything has been misrepresented to us. We would not have come if we knew how unwelcome we would be. If we had enough money we'd get out."[66] Within the hour he was handed a small amount of money for a train ticket, which he immediately returned to the City Marshal, George Schenck.

Ichiro Kawamoto returned to his wife about thirty minutes after he had been forcefully taken away. Two men and a woman from the mob escorted him. The woman was Mrs. Inez Riggs of Devitt. She was in Toledo that day visiting her daughter, Mrs. A.M. Wirfs.[67] Mrs. Riggs later recalled that from what she could see at the time, Mr. Kawamoto was not injured. She also commented on Mrs. Kawamoto, "This lady being so nervous and frightened, we went in [to her house]. I told her they needn't be frightened, that nobody was going to hurt them. She didn't seem to understand much."[68] Not all of the women in attendance were as kind. As Mrs. Kawamoto began preparing to leave, an unknown woman came up and started jerking laundry off of her clothesline. She threw the laundry at Mrs. Kawamoto saying, "Here, you forgot something."[69] Mrs. Kawamoto already had every intention of leaving.

A man and young woman came by the Kawamoto's house at this time and noticed the Kawamoto family dog. "I had a pup three months old," Ichiro later related. "I paid fifteen dollars for it. A white man and young lady came along and admired it. "This is a pretty nice dog" the man said and then took it. "You won't need the dog anyway because you're going to be killed in a few minutes."[70] Although the Sheriff was present, people continued threatening the *Issei*.

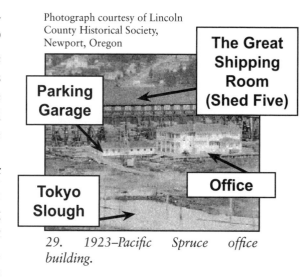

Photograph courtesy of Lincoln County Historical Society, Newport, Oregon

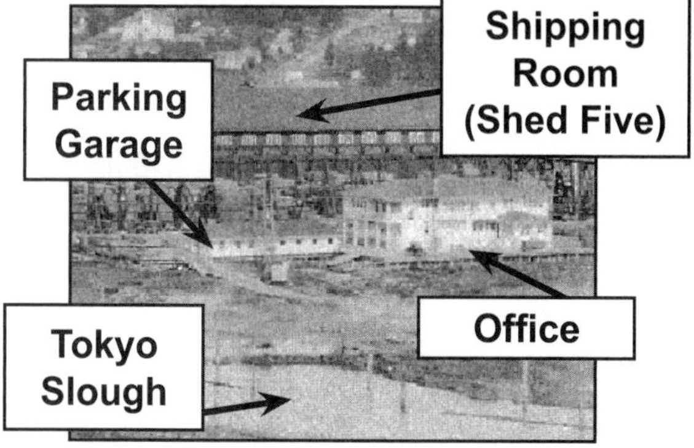

29. 1923–Pacific Spruce office building.

Lack of resistance by the Japanese during the riot most likely saved lives. Any of the *Issei* could easily have fought back with passion and anger. However, if they had put up a fight, there could have been further consequences, since the mob had a handgun and was initially out of control. Although all of the Asian employees were intimidated and insulted, Ichiro Kawamoto was the only one physically attacked (although Tamakichi Ogura was knocked to the ground).

From the Pacific Spruce Mill office (Photograph 29) C.D. Johnson and the other mill officials kept a close watch on the activities taking place, Johnson recognized the determination of the protesters attacking the Japanese:

> Forty-five minutes later we saw the mob marching the Japanese in a sort of squad, down the track. People were cursing in the crowd as they herded the Japanese out of the houses. People on the platform cheered [as the Japanese walked by], and then they followed.[71]

Johnson saw the Japanese driven like cattle to Hill Street (Main Street today) where cars and trucks were waiting to take them out of Lincoln County to Corvallis. Mr. Wirfs, a member of the mob, helped carry bags from the Japanese housing to the waiting vehicles. At the 1926 trial, he stated that there was a lot of luggage, and he wanted to hurry up the expulsion.[72]

Deputy Daniels re-arrested Germer. This time he was put in the jailhouse and remained incarcerated until later that evening (most likely to sober up). Four other people were also detained and charged with participation in a riot: W.S. Colvin, C. Buck, H.T. Pritchard and James Stewart.[73]

As Deputy Daniels locked the jailhouse door, a group from the mob confronted him. Morris Adderson of Siletz demanded the jail keys. Daniels, who was firm and calm, refused to give them up and said, "I have seven bullets and when they are gone, and I am dead, you can take them."[74] That ended the argument. All but Germer were later released on their own recognizance. These arrests provided some of the names that were used in the lawsuit the following year.

The cars and trucks used to transport the Japanese had been hastily arranged along Hill Street. One of the rioters, a Toledo farmer named H. A. Schlecht, went ahead of the Japanese to arrange for transportation with the Fred Horning Transfer Company to carry passengers and luggage. He commented later about his action, "I just took it on myself to order the trucks and I went to town to get [them]."[75] George Parrish, a lifelong resident of Toledo, recalled in a 2004 interview that his father, who was one of the truck drivers, told him that Fred Horning donated at least two trucks to transport the Japanese.[76] Another Horning Transfer employee who drove the Japanese was Howard (Smitty) S. Day. Day testified at the trial the following year that City Marshal Schenck had paid him twenty dollars to take the Japanese baggage and some of the Japanese to Corvallis located about fifty miles inland. Schenck handed Day the money and said sarcastically that the driving services should be donated.[77]

Prior to loading all of the *Issei* into the vehicles, A.R. Richardson passed a hat around to collect money. He reasoned that the money could be used by the Japanese to purchase train tickets from Corvallis to Portland.[78] When he attempted to turn over the collection, Mr. Koichi Yamano, refused to take it. His wife, Kazu took the money and passed it to Ogura who then gave it to City Marshal Schenck. Ogura told Schenck, "We don't want that kind of money," and suggested that Schenck give it to a charity.

Schenck then "shoved" Ogura and two other *Issei* into an automobile driven by a one armed man.[79] A. M. Wirfs also passed a hat around and collected over fifteen dollars and then gave the money to Ichiro Kawamoto. Like Yamano, Kawamoto returned the collection to City Marshal Schenck.[80] The total in these two hats was thirty dollars and thirty-six cents.[81] Mr. Youjiro Mitani was one of the Japanese loaded onto a truck. He commented at the trial that his driver, "drove recklessly and with an abandon and carelessness that caused …great alarm..."[82] In 1925, the road to Corvallis had hundreds of curves and it didn't take much speed to create a wild ride in the back of one of those old wooden trucks. During all of this confusion Mr. Mitani lost his watch which was valued at twenty-seven dollars.

Owen and Rollie Hart both offered to take people to Corvallis in their cars. Owen later insisted that no force was used to get the Japanese to ride with him. He shared cigarettes and had friendly conversation during the drive and noticed that his passengers seemed frightened. Owen later commented, "When we reached Corvallis they got out of the car and thanked me for bringing them."[83]

In all, twenty-two Japanese resident laborers, four Filipino employees, one Korean worker, two women and three Japanese American children were loaded into cars and trucks and driven to Corvallis.[84] Long-time Toledo resident Sid Neal was only five-years-old in 1925. He still remembers the image of that day quite vividly:

> They ran the Japanese out of Tokyo..., which was a housing area, located west of the mill across from Tokyo Slough. The houses were built on pilings. At that time we lived on the highway about three miles from town. When the procession passed by our house we came out to watch. Dad said, "well, that's the Japanese that are leaving." There was car after car and there were some trucks. I remember seeing their possessions loaded on top of the cars.[85]

As the vehicles reached the Corvallis train depot and people unloaded their belongings, some of the Japanese shook hands with their drivers and others said they were going to sue the Pacific Spruce Corporation for bringing them into the hostile town.[86]

Arrangements were made with the Southern Pacific agent for emergency transportation to Portland.[87] Twenty-four of the *Issei* left on a chartered Red Electric train that night. After arriving in Portland, they stayed at the Takatsugu Misao Hotel on SW 2nd, in downtown Portland. The hotel was owned by the Hasegawa Business Store.[88] That night they talked about what had just occurred and what they should do next.[89] A number of the men soon found work at sawmills located in Columbia County north of Portland.[90]

On Thursday following the riot the editor of the *Yaquina Bay News* wrote:

> While there is generally a very strong antipathy throughout the county against Japanese laborers being brought to work in the Spruce Corporation mill in any capacity, yet in this instance they were here and with the approval of an organized commercial body familiar with the situation, and that mob law was resorted to and the Stars and Stripes desecrated is resented and deeply deplored by all law abiding citizens.[91]

The outrage in this editorial indicates that many people were disgusted by the events of that day.

A short time after the riot, the Pacific Spruce Corporation hired a team of Mennonites to replace the *Issei* crew on the green-chain nightshift. A company security force was also organized for the protection of company property.[92]

NOTES

[1]Southern Pacific Time Table for 1925.

[2]Toledo Japanese Deportation, *Oregon Voter,* 12 Sept 1925, 385.

[3]Louis Powers, Telephone interview by author, Irrigon, Oregon July 6 2004.

[4]*Sovereigns of Themselves: A Liberating History of Oregon and Its Coast.* M. Constance Guardino III and Reverend Marilyn A. Riedel, 2002, p. 37.

[5]"Case L9710," *National Archives-Pacific AK Region,* Seattle, Washington.

[6]"Census: Japanese Population of Oregon," Bureau of Labor, Salem, Oregon, 1929.

[7]"Case L9713", *National Archives-Pacific AK Region, Seattle, Washington.*

[8]"Japanese Wins $2500 Damages," *The Morning Oregonian,* 24 July 1926.

[9]In 1925 the Toledo Chief of Police was called the City Marshal.

[10]"Schenck Denies That He Threatened Japs, "*Lincoln County Leader,* 8 Oct 1925.

[11]"The Toledo Incident," *The Great Northern Daily News,* Seattle, Washington, 29 July 1926.

[12]"Japanese Charge Threats to Kill," *The Morning Oregonian,* 14 July 1926.

[13]"Toledo Riot Defendant Tells Story," *The Capital Journal* , 16 July 1926.

[14]"Toledo Scene of Riot," *Yaquina Bay News*, 16 July 1925.

[15]"Toledo Riot Defendant Tells Story," *Journal.*

[16]"Toledo Defendant Target of Hot Quiz," *The Oregon Daily Journal* 16 July 1926.

[17]"Witnesses Tell of Cry for Blood," *The Oregon Daily Journal,* 14 July 1926.

[18]"Witnesses Tell," *Journal.*

[19]"Witnesses Tell," *Journal.* The author was not able to locate information regarding an incident at Longview.

[20]"Japanese Damage Suit Progresses," *Lincoln County Leader,* 22 July 1926.

[21]Toledo Scene of Riot," *Yaquina Bay News.*

[22]"Employee Of Pacific Spruce Corporation Condemns 'Agitators', *Lincoln County Leader,* 23 July 1925.

[23]"Toledo Scene of Riot," *Yaquina Bay News.*

[24]*Sovereigns of Themselves: A Liberating History of Oregon and Its Coast.* M. Constance Guardino III and Reverend Marilyn A. Riedel, 2002, p. 37.

[25]"Blames Boy for Toledo Racial Row," *The Oregon Daily Journal,* 20 July 1926.

[26]"Women Describe Riot at Toledo," *The Oregon Daily Journal,* 15 July 1926.

[27]"Mob Attack on Japanese is Described, *The Oregon Daily Journal,* 13 July 1926.

[28]"Toledo Mob Run Japs Out of Lincoln County," *Newport Journal,* 15 July 1925.

[29]"Witnesses Tell," *Journal.*

[30]"Riot at Toledo," *The Morning Oregonian,* 15 July 1926.

[31]"Witnesses Tell," *Journal.*

[32]"Case L9710," *National Archives.*

[33]Larry Hart, interview by author, written notes, Toledo, Oregon, May 20, 2004.

[34]"Toledo riot suit to go to verdict," *The Oregon Daily Journal,* 15 July 1926.

[35]"Japanese Charge, "*Morning Oregonian.*

[36]"Witnesses Tell," *Journal.*

[37]"Mob Attack on Colony Described," *The Oregon Daily Journal,* 13 July 1926.

[38]"Defense Denies Violence in Eviction of Japanese," *The Oregon Statesman,* 17 July 1926.

[39]"Jap suits against Toledo citizens opened Monday in Federal Court

at Portland," *Lincoln County Leader*, 15 July 1926.

[40]"Blames Boy," *Journal*.

[41]Larry Hart, interview by author, written notes, Toledo, Oregon, May 20, 2004.

[42]"Witnesses Tell," *Journal*.

[43]"Jap" suits against Toledo citizens opened Monday in Federal Court at Portland," *Lincoln County Leader*, 15 July 1926.

[44]"Toledo Defendant Target of Hot Quiz," *The Oregon Daily Journal*, 16 July 1926.

[45]"Argument in Toledo Case is underway," *The Oregon Daily Journal*, 22 July 1926.

[46]"Japanese Charge," *Morning Oregonian*.

[47]"Japanese Damage Suit Progresses; End of trial seen," *Lincoln County Leader*, 22 July 1926.

[48]"Jap Suits Against Toledo Citizens Opened Monday in Federal Court at Portland," *Lincoln County Leader*, 15 July 1926.

[49]"Toledo Riot Defendant Tells Story," *Capital Journal*, 16 July 1926.

[50]"Toledo Witnesses," *The Morning Oregonian*, 20 July 1926.

[51]"The Toledo Incident,"*The Great Northern Daily News*, 20 July 1926.

[52]"Toledo Scene of Riot," *Yaquina Bay News*.

[53]"Toledo Defense Denies Violence," *The Morning Oregonian*, 17 July 1926.

[54]"Japanese Tell of Labor Riot," *The Oregon Statesman*, 15 July 1926.

[55]"Witnesses Tell," *Journal*.

[56]"Witnesses Tell," *Journal*.

[57]"Japanese Describe Riot at Toledo," *The Morning Oregonian*, 15 July 1926.

[58]"'Jap' Suits Against Toledo Citizens Opened Monday in Federal Court at Portland," *Lincoln County Leader*, 15 July 1926.

[59]"Case L9711," *National Archives Pacific AK Region*, Seattle, Washingtion.

[60]"Japanese Damage Suit Progresses; End of Trial Seen," *Lincoln County Leader*, 22 July 1926.

[61]"Japanese Charge Threats to Kill," *The Morning Oregonian*, 14 July 1926.

[62]"Japanese Charge Threats to Kill," *Oregonian*.

[63]"Japanese Charge Threats to Kill," *Oregonian*.

[64]"Japanese Charge Threats to Kill," *Oregonian*.

[65]"'Jap' Suits Against Toledo," *Leader*.

[66]"Japanese Damage Suit Progresses",*Leader*.

[67]Devitt was a Hamlet logging community located along the Southern Pacific Railroad going from Toledo to Corvallis.

[68]"Toledo Defense Denies Violence," *Oregonian*.

[69]"Japanese Charge Threats to Kill," *Oregonian*.

[70]"Japanese Charge Threats to Kill," *Oregonian*.

[71]"'Jap' Suits Against Toledo," *Leader*.

[72] "Toledo Defense Denies Violence," *Oregonian*.

[73]"Japanese Charge Threats to Kill," *The Morning Oregonian,* 14 July 1926.

[74]"Toledo Scene of Riot," *Yaquina Bay News*.

[75]"Toledo Defense Denies Violence," *Oregonian*.

[76]George Parrish, taped interview by Author, Toledo, Oregon April 28, 2004.

[77]"Witnesses Tell," *Journal*.

[78]"Chief Puts Laugh in Gloomy Trial," *The Oregon Daily Journal,* 21 July 1926.

[79]"'Jap' Suits Against Toledo Citizens Opened Monday in Federal Court at Portland," *Lincoln County Leader,* 15 July 1926.

[80]"Toledo Defense Denies Violence," *Oregonian*.

[81]"Japanese invasion of Toledo Denied," *Corvallis Gazette-Times,* 24 July 1925.

[82]"Case L9711," *National Archives-Pacific AK Region,* Seattle, Washington.

[83]"Toledo Witnesses," *The Morning Oregonian,* 20 July 1926.

[84]"Twenty some Japanese were evicted from Lincoln County," *The Great Northern Daily News,* 13 July 1925.

[85]Sid Neal, interview by author, tape recording, Toledo, Oregon, May 20, 2004.

[86]"Toledo Citizens Tell Their Side of Ouster Case," *The Oregon Daily Journal,* 17 July 1926.

[87]"Japanese Workers Deported by Mob," *Corvallis Gazette-Times,* 13

July 1925. This account also says that four of the Japanese laborers left Toledo for Corvallis the next day (July 13th). The article does not explain why these four people were separated from the main group forced to leave by car on July 12th.

[88]"Twenty-some Japanese Evicted . . ." *The Great Northern Daily News*, 13 July 1925. Portland Directory-1925. [The Southern Pacific Red Electric Passenger Train was an interurban train that ran from Corvallis to Portland in 1925).

[89]"Toledo Incident," *The Great Northern Daily News,* 13 July 1925.

[90]"Japanese Win the First Skirmish in Big Damage Suit," *Lincoln County Leader,* 10 July 1925.

[91]"Toledo Scene of Riot," *Yaquina Bay News.*

[92]"Toledo Japanese Deportation," *Oregon Voter.*

Chapter 5: The Aftermath

1925
Tempest in a Teapot

On Sunday, July 12, 1925, the Toledo Police Department failed to perform its duty. This is due to the City Marshal's participation in removing Japanese labor from Toledo, an act (according to the *Oregon Voter*), that was both morally and legally indefensible.[1]

Within hours after the deportation, William A. Delzell (private secretary to Governor Walter M. Pierce), Charles H. Gram (State Labor Commissioner) and W. H. Fitzgerald (Deputy Labor Commissioner) drove to Toledo at the governor's request to investigate the matter. That evening, they interviewed members of the Lincoln County Protective League and on Monday the three men interviewed mill officials before returning to Salem.[2] There is no indication that they attempted to contact any of the victims. The following day they announced their hasty conclusion that the conflict would adjust itself as the emotions of the day subsided.[3]

Action was taken within Pacific Spruce Corporation. Retribution was swift and dealt some of the riot supporters a harsh blow. On Monday July 13, managers were given directions to "clean the mill." To do this they interviewed all of the employees.[4] Allen Green, an electrician and maintenance man was approached and asked, "Well, Mr. Green, what did you think about the fight yesterday?" He answered, "I wasn't there and I don't think anything about it."[5] He had gone fishing the day before with his two sons, Roy and Bill, and so he wasn't in town when the riot took place. Every employee was approached in a similar way. If they spoke up in support of the mob's actions, they were fired.

In addition, mill employees were told to stay away from the Pritchard Mercantile Company (located on Toledo's waterfront). Storeowner H.T. Pritchard was the mob spokesman on the day of the riot, and the corporate boycott forced him out of business.[6] At the civil trial in July, 1926 Pritchard complained bitterly that mill employees were fired if caught shopping at his store.

On the day of the riot, Pacific Spruce officials said they would prosecute the mob leaders, but general manager Frank W. Stevens announced the following week that corporate executives had changed their minds.[7] Mill management wanted to focus on business operations and determined that legal matters should remain in the hands of local government. However, to ensure future protection of company property, they decided to form a security force called the Pacific Spruce Law Enforcement League.[8]

Lincoln County District Attorney, E. P. Conrad, was not eager to pursue a criminal investigation. He announced that there would be no grand jury called to review the issue:

> In as much as no one was seriously injured, and that no attempt was made to harm the Japanese, that no property was destroyed and that the Pacific Spruce officials were not insisting upon prosecutions, the district attorney's office will not prosecute those arrested.[9]

For the time being, the Lincoln County district attorney was content to let things stand.

On Monday, July 13, Mrs. Rosemary Schenck led a delegation of the Lincoln County Protective League on a visit to the governor. Members of this group included: Mr. and Mrs. Leo Bateman, Mrs. Alice Waugh, Miss Verne Ross, Carl Brekke, Rev. C. Morris and Attorney R. M. Turner, their legal advisor.[10] Mrs. Schenck asked Governor Pierce for help in preventing the return of the Japanese to Toledo and added, "The large majority of citizens of Toledo and Lincoln County are opposed to the employment of Japanese laborers. But we are opposed to mob rule."[11] Her statement about opposing mob rule was in stark contrast to the inflammatory speech she had made just two days earlier at the ballpark.

The Lincoln County Protective League delegation told Governor Pierce that no mill workers were involved in the expulsion. Members of the league also alleged that Pacific Spruce Corporation only wanted to hire cheap labor at the mill, "which deprived many citizens of Toledo and the county a chance of livelihood."[12] Their comment indicates that the league was concerned that the hiring of Japanese labor was the first step in undercutting local wages and lowering the standard of living.

Ed Stack, Secretary of the State Federation of Labor, accompanied the Lincoln County Protective League delegation. Stack complained to Governor Pierce that the Pacific Spruce Corporation had pressured the State Chamber of Commerce to lobby Toledo businessmen on behalf of the Japanese in Toledo. Stack also told the Governor he had previously met with Mr. Hisakichi Okamoto, the Japanese consul in Portland, to request that the Japanese laborers be told to stay away from Toledo. Okamoto assured him that he had advised his countrymen not to return to Toledo since they were not wanted there. Okamoto also mentioned that he had been told the Pacific Spruce Corporation considered the hiring of Japanese labor good business since many of the orders for spruce came from Japan.[13]

Also visiting the governor on Monday, July 13 was Mr. W. G. Ide, Chairman of the Land Settlement Department of the Oregon State Chamber of Commerce. He tried to downplay the emotional impact and political significance of the riot by referring to the deportation as a "tempest in a teapot."[14] From the victims' perspective, however, the matter was far from over.

Although Governor Pierce listened to the delegation, he made no promises to the LCPL. A news article published in the *Oregon Statesman* the following day explained the Governor's position:

> There is no state official with power to take any action and it is doubtful if the federal authorities will interfere as long as the Japanese are in this country lawfully and committeed [sic] no crimes, it was said yesterday by men who refused to be quoted. As long as the Pacific Spruce Corporation lives up to its contract with the government no action can be taken.[15]

Judging by their visit to Governor Pierce's office, the Lincoln County Protective League remained naive about the rights of the Japanese residents to live wherever they wanted.

Although much of the information used to reconstruct this story is taken from American newspaper accounts, there were three *Issei* newspapers printed in the Pacific Northwest in 1925: *The Oregon News (Oshu Nippo)*, published in Portland, *The North American Times (Hokubei Jiji)*, published in Seattle and *The Great Northern Daily News (Taihoku Nippo)*, also published in Seattle. All three newspapers most likely covered the Toledo Incident, allowing their readers unfamiliar with printed English to follow events in their native language. Only copies of *The Great Northern Daily News* (Photograph 30) survive to verify this.

Image courtesy of University of Washington Libraries, Special Collections.

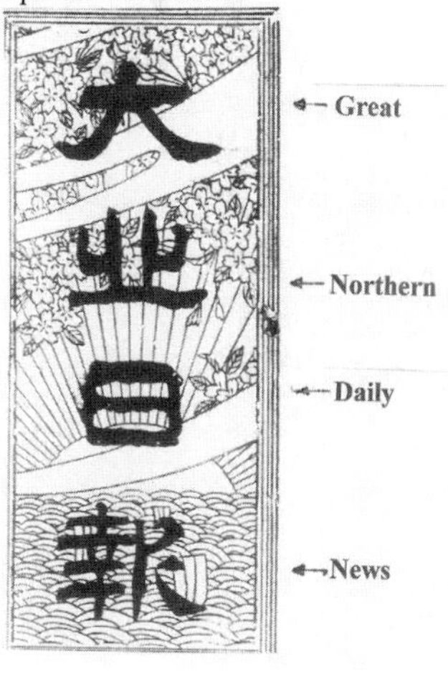

30. The Great Northern Daily News *was published six days a week.*

The Great Northern Daily News was published from 1909

to 1942, and had a contributing branch office in Portland. The newspaper covered the events in Toledo much as other newspapers in the Northwest did. Translations of several articles are included in the following chapters and provide contemporary *Issei* perspectives to the events occurring in 1925 and 1926.

The day after the riot an article appeared in *The Great Northern Daily News* (*Taihoku Nippo*) (Translation #1).

Translation by Hiroko Takada Amick and Glen-Paul Amick.

Translation #1
(See Appendix C for original Japanese)
The Great Northern Daily News
(Taihoku Nippo)
July 13, 1925

Twenty-some Japanese Evicted from Lincoln County.
Mob of 400 goes to Mill and Beats up Company Guards.
Tensions High past Several Weeks

A dispute brewing the last several weeks between Pacific Spruce Corporation in Toledo, Oregon and some workers over the hiring of Japanese for the mill, turned violent last Saturday with a bloody fist fight. A mob gathered up the Japanese and packed them with their belongings into cars and trucks and took them out of Lincoln County.

Before the mob rushed to the company, they held a meeting on the street. The leader of the mob gave a rousing speech to the gathering of some 400 people, including women and children. One American standing before the mob was waving the American Flag and then led the mob to the Japanese quarters.

The armed security guards employed by the company met the mob and spoke with the leaders, warning them not to enter company property. However, the mob paid no heed and engulfed the guards, disarming them and throwing their firearms away. Fighting broke out between the mob and the guards, with blood spilled on both sides, but only via fist fighting, not by guns.

The President of the company, C.D. Johnson and other company workers tried to talk reason to the mob, but the mob drowned them out. Before long the leader of the mob headed toward where the Japanese were and told them to put their belongings together in the cars and trucks and get out of the county.

The Japanese did not dare put up any resistance and left obediently.

Sheriff Horsfall rushed to the scene of the crime with his deputies and arrested three men, Martin Germer, Charles A. Buck and W.S. Colvin and ordered the people to disperse, which the mob reluctantly did.

The Sheriff wrote down the names of more than fifty active participants for punishment, with some going to jail.

Pacific Spruce Corporation announced a plan to hire Japanese people to work on the so-called "green-chain gangs" at their mill several weeks ago, as it was not possible to hire white workers at the normal pay rate for this work.

Strong opposition to this announcement formed, but some fifteen Japanese came from Portland last Thursday amid the tension. Although the company discussed the issue with the police and businessmen in the county, they couldn't see eye to eye.

But according to our reporter, the scoop above was published in the Oregonian. . . it was reported in the [*Portland Telegram*] and run on page 8 of the June 29 edition of this paper that the Toledo Chamber of Commerce and the Business Association of the Chamber held a meeting on the night of the 26 about the issue of hiring Japanese. As a result of lengthy discussions they reached an agreement to hire Japanese workers.

The Corporation employs over one thousand people and C.D. Johnson is the number one taxpayer in the county. He said that this was a sad incident, but that the company was not at fault and had to hire the Japanese to finish this job.

According to reports on the 12 in the [Toledo] newspaper, the mob numbered two hundred and fifty people.

A call from a branch to the head offices was received about eleven this morning stating that twenty-two Japanese, one Korean, and four Filipino, for a total of 27 workers, were run out of town.

They were sent to Corvallis, which is about fifty miles away, by car, with their belongings following on trucks. From Corvallis they took the train to Portland and are now staying at the Hasegawa Business Store in Portland and talking about what they are going to do next. They are likely to sue the Pacific Spruce Corporation.

Mr. Ide, Secretary of the State Chamber of Commerce, Governor Pierce and Senator McNary will meet to discuss the incident in Salem this morning.

It has been suggested that the riot did not stem from a racial problem, but because there were many white people who were looking for work in Toledo, the Company did not need to bring other workers from outside.

Similar to their occidental [western] counterparts, *Issei* correspondents were interested in bringing the dramatic aspects of an event to life for their readers.

Three days after the riot *The Great Northern Daily News* printed the following editorial concerning the deportation (Translation #2).

Translation by Hiroko Takada Amick and Glen-Paul Amick.

Translation #2
(See Appendix C for original Japanese)
The Great Northern Daily News
(Taihoku Nippo)
Wednesday July 15, 1925
Japanese Expulsion Incident

No solution has been found to the mob incident at Toledo, Oregon, which involved twenty-two Japanese, one Korean and four Filipino workers. (News from Tokyo yesterday mistakenly reported that 35 people were involved). The Salem newspaper reported on July 14th that State Labor Commissioner Mr. C. H. Gram gave Governor Pierce to understand that the trouble between white workers and company officials would likely be resolved peacefully.

Although it has not been made clear how a peaceful solution can be accomplished, it cannot be called a reasonable settlement unless the mob and its leader are punished sufficiently and the outcast Japanese are compensated for their damages. Further, considerable attention should be paid to this, so that such an incident does not reoccur, and if something like this should happen again, a guarantee should be in place that the police will offer reasonable protection.

Failing these things—if the mob is not called to account, if the Japanese are not compensated and future security is not assured—it would be fair to say that the rights of the Japanese have been completely ignored.

Some have suggested that this expulsion was not racially motivated, but that the Japanese got caught up in the conflict between the white workers and the company. The company claims that the reason they hired the Orientals was to perform work that white workers disdain, namely the "green-chain." If the company did not hire the Orientals, there would be no one to do the work and the company would struggle to operate. Also, according to claims of the mob, there are more than enough white workers and the company hires the Orientals in an effort to lower their wages in the future.

We don't know which argument is true, the company's or the white workers', but in either case, if new workers are brought in from outside the area, they should all be expelled, regardless of whether they are white or Japanese.

Situations such as last year, when strikebreakers from the Oriental Trading Company were expelled from the railroad strike in Auburn, Washington, should be dealt with as economic issues and not as racial. If it is a case like Turlock, California last year, in which Japanese jobs were taken away by white workers, we should deal with it as a racial matter.

The Japanese workers who were expelled from Toledo were not hired as strikebreakers, so we cannot just overlook them being unfairly run out of the county under threat of force.

The only bright spots in this dark affair was that it was not conducted violently and as the Japanese readily agreed to leave, some members of the mob felt badly and came up with a contribution toward the cost of traveling and gave it to the Japanese. The fact that the Japanese did not accept the money, asking that it be donated to a charity group instead, calls to mind Sadato and Yoshiie exchanging poetry at the battle of Koromogawa or the compassion of Kumagaya for Atsumori in the Gempei War at Su ma. The heroic tale perpetuates itself.

If the Japanese, like the company guards, had not acquiesced and left town peacefully at the time, one can easily imagine the mob would have expelled them forcibly through violence. The kind words the mob used at first in demanding the Japanese leave were in the end nothing but a threat. We should not miss the overall picture of a coerced expulsion because of a noble story in the middle of it.

We Japanese residents in the Pacific Rim and other regions have already been denied by law from working in agriculture. Now we are being denied the right to work in factories by intimidation. How will we make a living in the future if they limit how we live?

According to news from Tokyo, the Japanese Ministry of Foreign Affairs does not take the situation seriously and is maintaining a neutral stance. Now as in the past, it is regrettable that incompetent government officials, in the guise of neutrality, do nothing about the problem and neglect their duty without shame. With such a Ministry of Foreign Affairs, we overseas residents cannot help but feel an abject hopelessness.

We, who have been putting up with all kind of inconveniences and been at such disadvantage as foreigners from the beginning, have no leg to stand on if the government of our country fails to protect our rights under treaty agreements.

When so many people are trying to make a fair and just living and are expelled under force of threat by a mob, if our government does not deem this to be a serious incident, leaving it to be handled by the foreign government, we cannot help but doubt whether we are under the protection of our government.

The author is very vocal about his belief that *Issei* are without champion or governmental support. However, Japanese Consul, Hisakichi Okamoto, interviewed the deportees involved in the incident and forwarded a report to the Japanese Ambassador in Washington, D. C.[16] He also sent a request to Governor Pierce asking for an investigation of the incident.[17] With these measures the consul was working through diplomatic channels to help his countrymen.

Nonetheless Japanese residents living along the West Coast were confronted with a variety of challenges such as those faced by the men and women thrown out of their homes on the Pacific Spruce property. The Toledo disturbance was part of a larger systemic problem known to those who live with fear and harassment because of their cultural and physical differences.

Eleven days after the deportation, Mr. Iwao Oyama,

Secretary of the Japanese Association of Oregon (Photograph 31) and publisher of the *Oregon News* (Photograph 32), wrote an article about the Toledo Incident, which was printed in the *Corvallis Gazette-Times*. In explaining the *Issei* point of view, Oyama pointed out that in June 1925, the Japanese Association of Oregon had been informed that there were no longer objections to the employment of the Japanese residents in Toledo, that all anti-Japanese sentiment was gone and that there would be no further trouble with the Toledo Chamber of Commerce. A Japanese employment agent was then hired to send laborers.

Photograph courtesy of
Albert A. Oyama family collection

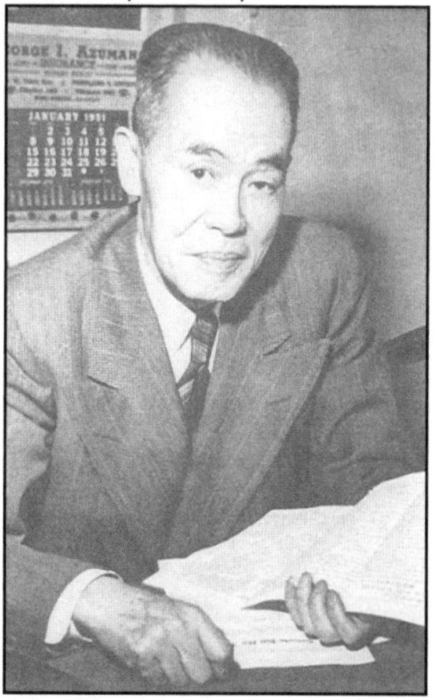

31. This photograph was taken in 1951, the year before Mr. Iwao Oyama died.

Newspaper logo courtesy
of Homer and Miki Yasui
family collection

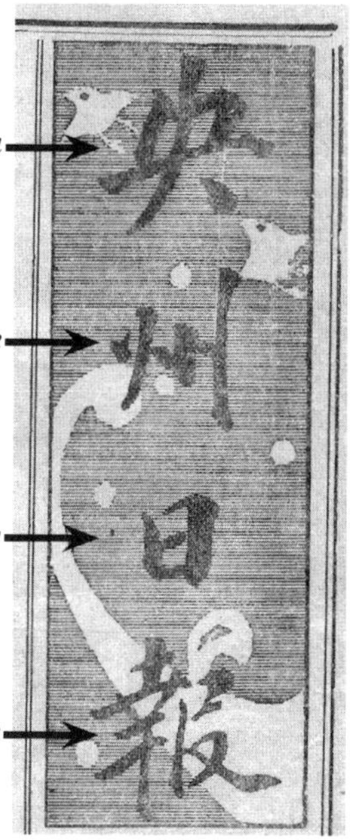

32. The Oregon News Logo–Portland, Oregon 1938.

Oyama went on to say that the Toledo protestors claimed that the Pacific Spruce mill was planning to pay the Japanese two dollars and sixty cents a day. He explained that there weren't any

Japanese mill workers in Oregon working for a wage that low. The agreement with the Pacific Spruce Corporation was four dollars per day for an eight-hour shift. Mr. Oyama also commented about the rough treatment the Japanese residents had received and about the personal property they lost.

With respect to the claim that the Japanese residents were given more than one hundred and twenty dollars from mob members before leaving Toledo, Oyama stated that the amount collected was, in truth, only thirty dollars and thirty-six cents and that the money was not accepted but turned over to the Toledo City Marshal.[18] His article went on to say:

> For our part, nothing is more deplorable than this unhappy incident. We rely on Governor Pierce and the righteous spirit of Toledo officials and the humane feeling and sound, common sense of its people, not only for the sake of the ousted Japanese, but also for the sake of civilized humanity and we hope that the question will see a happy solution.[19]

Oyama's hope would prove to be in vain.

The Japanese Association of Oregon was not the only group investigating the incident. About three weeks after the riot, the Portland Council of Churches (a strong multi-denominational group organized in 1919)[20] appointed a special committee of five to investigate the Toledo Incident. They surveyed newspaper accounts, conducted interviews with all of the parties involved and went on a fact-finding trip to Toledo.[21]

Six weeks after their inquiry began, the Council of Churches presented its results in three parts: a chronology of events leading to the deportation of the Japanese residents, comments on facts gathered during the investigation and recommendations regarding the riot. The report pointed out that equal protection by American law is guaranteed to all resident aliens and that Toledo law enforcement failed to protect the Japanese laborers while they were in Toledo. If the Toledo Police Department had chosen to be in control on July 12, 1925 the abuse of innocent mill employees would not have occurred. The committee found it disturbing that racial prejudice and the perceived threat of job loss were used as excuses to justify the deportation of innocent Japanese men and women.[22]

The report published in the *Oregon Voter* (Photograph 33)[23] also discussed the issue of prejudice and job security on a statewide level:

> The average citizen of Toledo, (or any other similarly situated community) whenever foreigners are mentioned in connection with his work, immediately thinks of low economic standards, poor living conditions, and low wages. He has heard unfavorable stories about Japanese laborers in this country. He knows that jobs are limited. When a group of strangers is transplanted wholesale into his community he naturally fears for his own future. The difference in color only augments his resentment. If Japanese laborers were gradually inducted into the mill community, taking their place in the various jobs and social activities alongside the whites, the same as any other new laborers, rather than segregated as strangers, they would soon be accepted as friends through the mere process of acquaintance. This has happened in other mills and no race "problem" has resulted.[24]

The Council's report suggested that when minority labor was introduced to an area one employee at a time, the individuals were more apt to be accepted into the community. A major problem in what occurred in Toledo, according to the Council of Churches point of view, was that the *Issei* came in large numbers and the people of Toledo were led to believe that the Japanese would be paid lower wages resulting in a loss of jobs and a lower standard of community life.

After the Japanese crew was evicted from Toledo, the

Courtesy of Valley Library, Oregon State University, Corvallis, Oregon

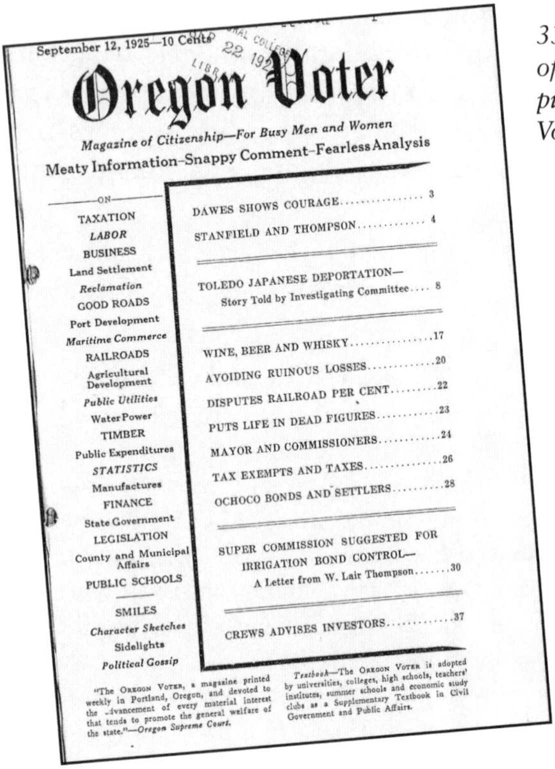

September 12, 1925—10 Cents

Oregon Voter

Magazine of Citizenship—For Busy Men and Women

Meaty Information-Snappy Comment-Fearless Analysis

—ON—

TAXATION
LABOR
BUSINESS
Land Settlement
Reclamation
GOOD ROADS
Port Development
Maritime Commerce
RAILROADS
Agricultural Development
Public Utilities
Water Power
TIMBER
Public Expenditures
STATISTICS
Manufactures
FINANCE
State Government
LEGISLATION
County and Municipal Affairs
PUBLIC SCHOOLS

SMILES
Character Sketches
Sidelights
Political Gossip

DAWES SHOWS COURAGE.............. 3
STANFIELD AND THOMPSON............ 4

TOLEDO JAPANESE DEPORTATION—
Story Told by Investigating Committee.... 8

WINE, BEER AND WHISKY..............17
AVOIDING RUINOUS LOSSES............20
DISPUTES RAILROAD PER CENT.........22
PUTS LIFE IN DEAD FIGURES..........23
MAYOR AND COMMISSIONERS............24
TAX EXEMPTS AND TAXES..............26
OCHOCO BONDS AND SETTLERS..........28

SUPER COMMISSION SUGGESTED FOR
IRRIGATION BOND CONTROL—
A Letter from W. Lair Thompson.......30

CREWS ADVISES INVESTORS............37

"The Oregon Voter, a magazine printed weekly in Portland, Oregon, and devoted to the advancement of every material interest that tends to promote the general welfare of the state."—*Oregon Supreme Court.*

Textbook—The Oregon Voter is adopted by universities, colleges, high schools, teachers' institutes, summer schools and economic study clubs as a Supplementary Textbook in Civil Government and Public Affairs.

33. Today the League of Women Voters® publishes the Oregon Voter.

Pacific Spruce Corporation hired a crew of Mennonites to work the same green-chain night shift for which the Japanese had been hired. There is no indication that any kind of protest was made against the new crew, even though the Mennonites were outsiders and not from Lincoln County.[25]

By September 1925, both the civil and criminal arms of the judiciary became involved. Criminal investigations had been stalled by apathy and arrogance but civil action was in motion as the deported *Issei* took a stand against the violation of their rights. On October 1, 1925, with the help of the Japanese Association of Oregon, five of the *Issei* involved in the riot filed separate actions against nine of the Toledo residents who were involved.[26]

One of the lawyers for the Japanese prosecution team, W. Lair Thompson, claimed that the *Issei* civil suits would establish a precedent for alien rights in the United States.[27]

Table 2. Brief biographies of the Plaintiffs.
Photographs courtesy of Valley Library, Oregon State University, Corvallis, Oregon

In 1926, Mr. Ichiro Kawamoto had been an Oregon resident more than eighteen years. Before going to Toledo he managed a hopyard near Salem, Oregon. Pacific Spruce Corporation hired Kawamoto as foreman for five dollars a day. He was authorized to assemble an *Issei* crew and bring them to Toledo.[28] Kawamoto was suing for twenty-five thousand dollars in damages.

In 1926 Tamakichi* Ogura had been an Oregon resident for ten years. Before coming to Toledo he worked at a hopyard in Multnomah, County.[29] He was hired by the Pacific Spruce Corporation for four dollars and fifty cents a day. Ogura was suing for twenty-five thousand dollars in damages.

In 1926, Matsuto Tsubokawa had been an Oregon resident for over six years. He was a farm worker when hired by the Pacific Spruce Corporation for three dollars and sixty cents a day.[30] He was suing for twenty-five thousand dollars in damages.

By 1926, Youjiro Mitani had been living in Oregon more than four years. He was a laundry worker prior to being hired by the Pacific Spruce Corp. for three dollars and sixty cents a day.[31] He was suing for twenty-five thousand dollars in damages. He died before the case was settled.

In 1926, Mrs. Ito Kawamoto, wife of Ichiro Kawamoto, had been an Oregon resident for over eighteen years. She was hired by Pacific Spruce Corporation to cook for three dollars a day for the crew.[32] She was suing for thirty thousand dollars in damages.

ITO KAWAMOTO (Photo not available)

*The language translators were not one hundred percent positive that Ogura's first name was Tamakichi, is could have been Tamayoshi.

The five lawsuits (Table 2) sought a total of one hundred and thirty thousand dollars in damages, not a lot of money by current standards but an astounding amount for a minority civil rights case in 1926.

On October 2, 1925 U.S. Marshal Clarence R. Hotchkiss and U.S. Deputy A. Johnson made a trip from Portland to Toledo to serve summonses (Photograph 34) to nine Toledo residents: George Schenck (Toledo City Marshal), William S. Colvin (owner of Colvin's General Store), Frank Sturdevant (farmer), Owen Hart (barber shop owner), Rosemary Schenck (community leader), Harry T. Pritchard (owner of Pritchard Mercantile), H. Germer, Charles A. Buck and L. D. Emerson.[33]

If the defendants had ignored the summonses there would have been an automatic judgment against the nine individuals for one hundred and thirty thousand dollars. Those served with a summons had thirty days to respond.

Courtesy of National Archives, Pacific AK Region, Seattle, Washington

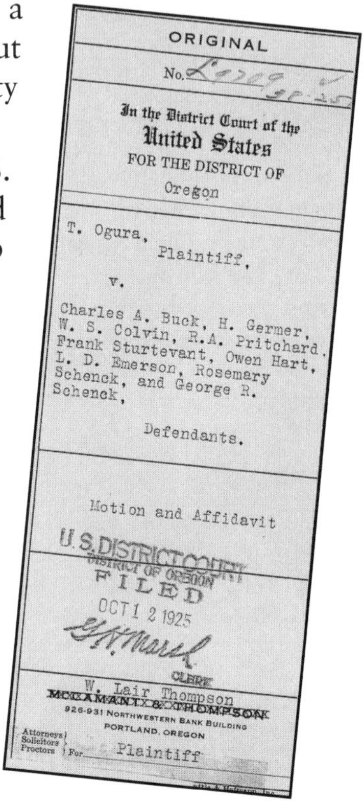

ORIGINAL

No.

In the District Court of the United States

FOR THE DISTRICT OF Oregon

T. Ogura,
Plaintiff,

v.

Charles A. Buck, H. Germer, W. S. Colvin, R.A. Pritchard, Frank Sturtevant, Owen Hart, L. D. Emerson, Rosemary Schenck, and George R. Schenck,
Defendants.

Motion and Affidavit

U.S. DISTRICT COURT
DISTRICT OF OREGON
FILED
OCT 1 2 1925
CLERK

W. Lair Thompson
McCAMANT & THOMPSON
926-931 NORTHWESTERN BANK BUILDING
PORTLAND, OREGON
Attorneys Solicitors Proctors For Plaintiff

34. Copy of Summons delivered in Toledo, Oregon, October 2, 1925.

The Lincoln County Protective League organizers had been in contact with Mr. Edward J. Stack from the State Federation of Labor since June. After the civil lawsuit was filed, they asked for his advice regarding a lawyer.[34] He recommended Portland Attorney B. A. Green.[35] Green had represented labor issues in Multnomah County since 1914 and wasted no time in publicly attempting to spin the charges in another direction and place blame for the riot squarely on the Pacific Spruce Corporation:

> I would like to make it clear that the issue is not as was announced when the suit was filed, that is one of whether foreigners in this country have protection under our laws. It is really whether a corporation can import foreign labor and break down the standard of living as was attempted in this case. I also wish to insist that the real plaintiff in this case is the Pacific Spruce Corporation and that the Japanese themselves are merely figureheads.[36]

Brushing aside the Japanese rights to protection under the law, Attorney Green insinuated that the Pacific Spruce Corporation hired the Japanese crew for wages lower than were paid currently, a claim that was never proven to be correct.

Organized labor in Oregon offered their support to the Toledo defendants.[37] By the middle of October 1925, Mr. Fred Ross, Manager of the Farm-Labor Legal Bureau, was in Toledo to organize a fundraising drive to help pay for trial costs:

> There is the possibility that people of Lincoln County are unaware of the seriousness of the cases that have been filed against citizens of Lincoln County because of the part they played in ousting the colony of Japanese...Each of the defendants is to be tried separately, the move being to make it just as expensive for each defendant as possible. The cases will establish a precedent...Therefore the very life of your community and the business welfare of the towns of Lincoln County are at stake.[38]

At Fred Ross's suggestion, the Lincoln County Protective League sent representatives to every part of the county asking for donations. Their goal was to ask every man and woman in the county for a donation to the "cause." According to newspaper accounts, all they were able to muster up was two hundred sixty-eight dollars. This small amount was a statement in itself. Many people may have been willing to sign a petition to keep *Issei* labor out of the county, but when push came to shove, they did not choose to get involved.

On October 29, Defense Attorney Green made a pre-trial motion that the Japanese should be required to put up cost bonds totaling twelve thousand dollars. The purpose of the cost bond is similar to posting bail, that is, money is placed into an independent account. If the person posting bond disappears without meeting his obligations, the money is forfeited. In the case of the cost bond, the money would go to paying court expenses for the Toledo defendants if they were to win the lawsuit. Green declared:

> Your honor, these people are aliens, they have no ties to hold them here and they can pack up and leave the country any time they want. There is nothing to hold them, and the defendants should be protected in the suit to the extent of having their costs protected.[39]

Attorney Green may have had a different motive for requesting the cost bond than the possible disappearance of the *Issei*. If the Judge were to agree to this motion, then in effect the Japanese residents would be declared non-residents of Oregon, possibly aiding the Toledo defense in winning the trial.

Green's request presented a problem for four of the five plaintiffs. By that time they had found work in Columbia County logging camps located north of Portland, far removed from a notary public. Taking time off from work to travel to Portland for the purpose of signing notarized affidavits would have been difficult. Fortunately, for the four working elsewhere, there was someone from the *Issei* community who could help. In 1925 Daiichi Takeoka was President of the Oregon Japanese Association (Photograph 35).

To counter Attorney Green's pre-trial request for the cost bond, Mr. Takeoka submitted through *Issei* attorney W.

Photograph courtesy of Homer and Miki Yasui family collection

35. (Charles) Daiichi Takeoka. Family portrait taken circa 1915.

Lair Thompson, four notarized affidavits to Judge Wolverton. The affidavits declared that Mr. Takeoka had known the plaintiffs: Matsuto Tsubokawa, Youjiro Mitani, Ichiro Kawamoto and Ito Kawamoto from four to eighteen years and during that time that they were all residents of Oregon (Photograph 36).[40] Tamakichi Ogura was in Portland at the time and was able to give his own sworn declaration.[41]

After reviewing the five *Issei* affidavits Judge Charles Wolverton overruled Attorney Green's bond motion on December 9, 1925. The Judge was satisfied that all of the Japanese plaintiffs were Oregon residents.[42]

While the *Issei* had been busy gathering affidavits in the civil trial, the Japanese government pushed for conclusion of the criminal investigation. On November 19, having waited for Oregon officials to take action on the evidence of rights' violations, the new Japanese Consul in Portland, Mr. K. Midzusawa, contacted Governor Pierce, demanding an update on the prosecution of those involved in the incident.[43] As a result of this pressure the governor contacted Lincoln County District Attorney E. P. Conrad in Toledo urging that the investigation be conducted as quickly as possible.

Courtesy of National Archives, Pacific AK Region, Seattle, Washington

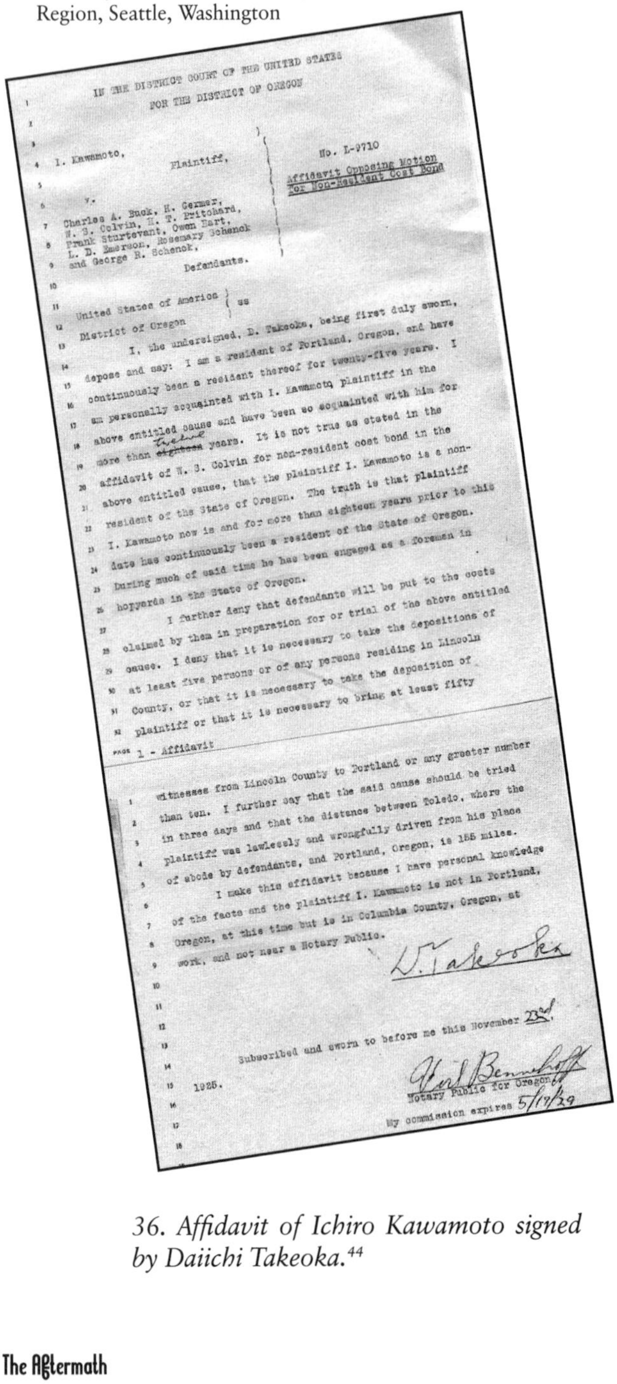

IN THE DISTRICT COURT OF THE UNITED STATES
FOR THE DISTRICT OF OREGON

I. Kawamoto,
Plaintiff,
v.
Charles A. Buck, H. Germer, W. S. Colvin, H. T. Pritchard, Frank Sturtevant, Owen Hart, L. D. Emerson, Rosemary Schenck and George R. Schenck,
Defendants.

No. L-9710

Affidavit Opposing Motion For Non-Resident Cost Bond

United States of America } ss
District of Oregon

I, the undersigned, D. Takeoka, being first duly sworn, depose and say: I am a resident of Portland, Oregon, and have continuously been a resident thereof for twenty-five years. I am personally acquainted with I. Kawamoto, plaintiff in the above entitled cause and have been so acquainted with him for more than ~~eighteen~~ twelve years. It is not true as stated in the affidavit of W. S. Colvin for non-resident cost bond in the above entitled cause, that the plaintiff I. Kawamoto is a non-resident of the State of Oregon. The truth is that plaintiff I. Kawamoto now is and for more than eighteen years prior to this date has continuously been a resident of the State of Oregon. During much of said time he has been engaged as a foreman in hopyards in the State of Oregon.

I further deny that defendants will be put to the costs claimed by them in preparation for or trial of the above entitled cause. I deny that it is necessary to take the depositions of at least five persons or of any persons residing in Lincoln County, or that it is necessary to take the deposition of plaintiff or that it is necessary to bring at least fifty

PAGE 1 - Affidavit

witnesses from Lincoln County to Portland or any greater number than ten. I further say that the said cause should be tried in three days and that the distance between Toledo, where the plaintiff was lawlessly and wrongfully driven from his place of abode by defendants, and Portland, Oregon, is 155 miles.

I make this affidavit because I have personal knowledge of the facts and the plaintiff I. Kawamoto is not in Portland, Oregon, at this time but is in Columbia County, Oregon, at work, and not near a Notary Public.

D. Takeoka

Subscribed and sworn to before me this November 23rd, 1925.

Notary Public for Oregon
My commission expires 5/17/29

36. *Affidavit of Ichiro Kawamoto signed by Daiichi Takeoka.*[44]

On November 30, 1925, District Attorney Conrad finally announced that the Toledo deportation case would go before the Grand Jury at the County Courthouse in Toledo during the February session.

Mr. W. Lair Thompson, one of the attorneys for the *Issei*, commented about the governor's request:

> I should not be surprised to find it turning into a propaganda to have a criminal trial in Toledo, where there is a chance of whitewash, rather than a civil trial in Portland, where there is a chance that the aliens might win their suit.[45]

From previous actions taken in Lincoln County, Attorney Thompson did not believe that a Lincoln County jury would be unbiased in hearing the case.

With Conrad's announcement of a pending Grand Jury investigation, the Toledo defendants were now struggling on two fronts. As the criminal investigation moved forward, pretrial motions continued in the first of five civil lawsuits.

After Judge Wolverton's December 10 ruling on the cost bond, Attorney Green presented his defense strategy for the upcoming trial:

> While it appears on the face that these Oriental laborers were being paid $4 each daily, we contend that they received only $2 each per day, the other $2 going to the Japanese labor boss who furnished the laborers. We will prove that the so-called mob was a crowd of Toledo people who went to the mill and explained in a perfectly quiet, law abiding manner to the Japanese that they were not desired, that a meeting had been held and the mill officers were told Orientals were not wanted. When this was explained, they went into their cabins, which had been furnished by the company and talked the matter over. Then they came out and said they would leave if transportation were furnished for them back to Portland. The Townspeople furnished. . . automobiles to Corvallis and money given

> the Japanese to pay their fares from Corvallis to Portland. There was not one speck of violence shown towards the Orientals, not one threat made to these Japanese workers by any member of the so-called mob.
>
> But here is where the violence came in; Johnson, the general manager and president of the company, rushed out with a revolver and made threats. He was promptly knocked over the head with a board and his revolver thrown into the lake. His son also came out with a gun, and another board tapped him on the head.
>
> Two other officers of the company appeared with revolvers; they were made immediately acquainted with the business side of two large boards and the four guns all were thrown into a nearby lake or pond. While we contend the Japanese were not hurt or threatened in any manner whatsoever, we do not make the same contention regarding Johnson and their other company officers who appeared with revolvers. I understand they were pretty badly mauled.[46]

Attorney Green's statement was incorrect on several points which would become obvious during the civil trial set to begin the following July.

Although District Attorney Conrad had not expected the Grand Jury to argue the Japanese case until February, the case was moved forward one month. The names of those on the grand jury were published in the local newspaper on

Table 3. Lincoln County Grand Jury, 1926.

R. H. Davis, Jury Foreman	Waldport
J. C. Fox	Alsea
G. M. Laughlin	Eddyville
Lorena Cook	Chitwood
Maurice Anderson	Siletz
Andrew Wisniewski	Kernville
Nels W. Miller	Elk City

Thursday, January 21, just four days before the jury was to convene (Table 3).[47]

Between that Thursday and the following Sunday, each member of the jury received an unsigned, threatening letter. The letter did not state that lives were at risk, but suggested that something bad would happen if jury members indicted the accused: "Should indictments be returned against those who ousted the Japanese, the question would be settled forever."[48] Although there isn't any direct evidence to suggest that this letter was taken seriously, the outcome of the jury's deliberation leaves room for speculation.

The Grand Jury convened in a closed-door hearing on January 25, 1926 to listen to the evidence and consider a criminal case. When they were done, they had not reached a consensus. The jury accomplished nothing more than to draw attention to the Toledo Incident. None of their proceedings were made public and no action was recommended.[49]

With the threat of criminal indictment behind them, the nine Toledo defendants focused on their defense for the upcoming civil suit.

NOTES

[1]"Toledo Japanese Deportation," *Oregon Voter,* (12 Sept 1925): 388.

[2]"State Officials Here Making Investigations on Japanese Affair," *Lincoln County Leader,* 16 July 1925.

[3]"Japanese Rumpus at Toledo Probed," *Oregon Statesman,* 14 July 1925.

[4]"Japanese Deportation," *Voter,* 386.

[5]Roy Green, interview by author, written notes, Corvallis, Oregon, January 15, 2004.

[6]"Japanese Tell of Labor Riot," *Oregon Statesman*, 15 July 1926.

[7]"Japanese Deported by Toledo Citizens Following Mass Meet," *Lincoln County Leader*, 16 July 1925.

[8]"Japanese Deportation," *Voter,* 385/391.

[9]"Japanese Deported by Toledo Citizens Following Mass Meet," *Lincoln County Leader*, 16 July 1925.

[10]"Japanese Deported," *Leader*.

[11]"Japanese Deported," *Leader*.

[12]"Case L9709," National Archives-Pacific AK Region, Seattle, Washington.

[13]"Japanese Rumpus at Toledo Probed," *Oregon Statesman*, 14 July 1925.

[14]"Japanese Workers Deported by Mob," *Corvallis Gazette-Times,* 13 July 1925.

[15] "Japanese Rumpus at Toledo Probed," *Oregon Statesman,* 14 July 1925.

[16]"Japanese Calm Over Oregon Mob Action," *The Oregon Daily Journal,* 14 July 1925.

[17]"No Action Taken," *Corvallis Gazette-Times,*14 July 1925.

[18]"Japanese Invasion of Toledo Denied," *Corvallis Gazette-Times,* 24 July 1925.

[19]"Japanese Invasion," *Corvallis Gazette-Times.*

[20]"EMO marks 30 years of service and unity," *Voice,* Feb 2004.

[21]"Extensive report made on ousting of Japanese at Toledo," *Lincoln County Leader,* 10 Sept 1925.

[22]The *Oregon Voter* is a magazine dedicated to active participation of citizens in government and public affairs since 1914.

[23]"Japanese Deportation," *Voter,* 388.

[24]"Japanese Deportation," *Voter,* 388.

[25]"Japanese Deportation," *Voter,* 385.

[26]"Grand Jury to Investigate Japanese Deportation, Says Report from Governor's Office," *Lincoln County Leader,* 3 Dec 1925.

[27]"Grand Jury," *Leader.*

[28]"Case L-9710," National Archives-Pacific AK Region, Seattle, Washington.

[29]"Case L-9709," National Archives-Pacific AK Region, Seattle, Washington.

[30]"Case L-9712," National Archives-Pacific AK Region, Seattle, Washington.

[31]"Case L-9711," National Archives-Pacific AK Region, Seattle, Washington.

[32]"Case L-9713," National Archives-Pacific AK Region, Seattle, Washington.

[33]"Case L-9709," National Archives-Pacific AK Region, Seattle, Washington.

[34]"Unions Aid Toledo defense," *Lincoln County Leader,* 8 Oct 1925.

[35]*Eminent Judges and Lawyers of the Northwest, 1843-1955.* C. W. Taylor Jr., 2898 Louis Road, Palo Alto, California. p 123.

[36]"Unions to aid Toledo defense," *Lincoln County Leader,* 8 Oct 1925.

[37]Although there were organized unions in Oregon prior to 1900, it was not until 1902 that the Oregon State Federation of Labor (a chapter of the American Federation of Labor, established 1886) held it's first state convention. The federation served as an umbrella organization throughout the state. It was active in pro-union legislation and worked heavily in advocating support for issues such as compulsory education and the eight-hour work day. The federation strived to win over public sentiment for its member unions.

[38]"Effort Being Made (to) Finance Local People in Japanese Fight," *Lincoln County Leader,* 22 Oct 1925.

[39]"Japanese Win the First Skirmish in Big Damage Suit," *Lincoln County Leader,* 10 Dec 1925.

[40]"Japanese Win," *Leader.*

[41]"Case L9713," National Archives Pacific AK Region, Seattle, Washington.

[42]"Japanese Win," *Leader.*

[43]"Grand Jury to Investigate Japanese Deportation, Says Report from Governor's Office," *Lincoln County Leader,* 3 Dec 1925.

[44]"Case L9710," National Archives Pacific AK Region, Seattle, Washington.

[45]"Grand Jury to Investigate," *Leader.*

[46]"Japanese Win the First Skirmish in Big Damage Suit," *Lincoln County Leader,* 10 Dec 1925.

[47]"130 Cases Make Up Circuit Court Docket for February Term," *Lincoln County Leader,* 21 Jan 1926.

[48]"Report Attempt Was Made to Intimidate the Grand Jury," *Lincoln County Leader,* 28 Jan 1925.

[49]"Grand Jury Fails to Indict Jap Deporter's," *Lincoln County Leader,* 28 Jan 1926.

Chapter 6:
Going to Trial

1926 - The First Civil Case of Its Kind To Be Tried In the United States

The Japanese Association of Oregon retained the law firm of McCamant and Thompson (legal advisors to the Pacific Spruce Corporation in other situations) to represent the *Issei*. They chose to use the 1911 Treaty of Commerce and Navigation between Japan and the United States as the basis of their lawsuit. This treaty guaranteed Japanese residents the right to reside and work within the U. S. under the protection of American law—including the *Issei* right to live in peace without fear of unlawful invasion of their property.[1] [The 1911 agreement remained in force until 1939. See Appendix A for further detail.]

Portland attorney B. A. Green (recommended to the defendants by Edward J. Stack, Secretary of the Oregon State Federation of Labor)[2] was the lead defense attorney. He was assisted by Leonard Krause and R. M. Turner of Toledo. The defense team held that the Japanese residents left Toledo on their own accord once several prominent Toledo citizens explained to the *Issei* workers that they were not welcome. The defense further argued that by bringing in the Japanese labor force, the Pacific Spruce Corporation violated a gentleman's agreement with the citizens of Toledo not to hire an outside labor force.[3] Finally, the defense contended that the defendants had acted in a peaceful manner and that the Japanese plaintiffs had misinterpreted their actions.

The trial started on a warm Monday morning July 12, 1926, exactly one year after the expulsion took place. The courtroom was already humid as the room filled to capacity with those who were to testify and those who went simply to observe.

When the case opened, plaintiff attorneys W. Lair Thompson and John Collier moved to dismiss charges against three of the defendants who were no longer in the area. Martin H. Germer, Charles A. Buck and L. D. Emerson had disappeared.[4] Since the U.S. Marshal's office was unable to locate the missing men in Toledo or other parts of Lincoln County, deputies could not serve the summonses. With all parties in agreement Judge Wolverton granted the motion. The suit continued against the remaining six defendants: W. S. Colvin, Harry T. Pritchard, Frank Sturdevant, Owen Hart, Rosemary Schenck and George R. Schenck (Photograph 37).

Photograph courtesy of Valley Library, Oregon State University, Corvallis, Oregon

37. Photograph taken on the courthouse steps in Portland during the 1926 trial. In the center, front row, are George Schenck, his son, Jack Schenck and Rosemary Schenck.[5]

The Great Northern Daily News carried the following description of the opening day's proceedings (Translation #3).

Translation by Hiroko Takada Amick and Glen-Paul Amick.

Translation #3

(See Appendix C for original Japanese text)

The Great Northern Daily News

(Taihoku Nippo)

July 13, 1926

Toledo Incident

First Day of Trial

(From the Portland Branch)

The damage claim suit brought by our countrymen over the eviction from Toledo by a mob there began, as reported, at the Federal Court under Judge Wolverton at 2 p.m. on the 12th. Lawyers for the plaintiff are Lair Thompson and Collier and the defendants are represented by lawyers Green, Krause and [Turner]. The 12 jurors were selected by 3 p.m..

Lawyer Thompson for the plaintiffs explained the eviction incident in detail to the jurors.

Attorney Green for the defendants protested to the jury that, in spite of its contract with the people of Toledo not to hire workers from outside the area if they do not form a labor union, the Company hired Japanese workers anyway. He also argued that the US-Japan Commercial Treaty was meant for commercial matters between the two countries, so the incident at hand should not be discussed with reference to the treaty.

Judge Wolverton disavowed the defendants' lawyer Mr. Green's interpretation of the treaty, saying that the US-Japan Commercial Treaty recognizes the right of continued residence for individuals and so naturally should protect their lives and property.

As a witness for the state, Sheriff Horsfall of Lincoln County took the witness stand and listed the names of some 50 people who he witnessed as the mob involved in the eviction incident.

The trial was adjourned at 4 p.m. and was to resume at 10 a.m. the following morning.

The reporter's reference to "our countrymen" expresses a sense of community felt by the *Issei*. Although many of the *Great Northern Daily News* readers did not personally know the individuals who were treated poorly by some of Toledo's citizens, the deported *Issei* were still part of a larger group held together by customs and ancestry. Japanese residents understood the challenge of integrating into a culture in which they were the minority.

The following day *The Great Northern Daily News* continued its coverage of the trial (Translation #4), bringing out the complex issues of rights, business and intent.

Translation by Hiroko Takada Amick and Glen-Paul Amick.

Translation #4
(See Appendix C for original Japanese text)
The Great Northern Daily News
(Taihoku Nippo)
July 14, 1926

Toledo Incident,
Second Day of Trial
(From the Portland Branch)

The trial resumed at two o'clock.

The plaintiff Ichiro Kawamoto took the witness stand and described the situation at the time in detail, saying that on July 12 last year, a mob of dozens of people carrying an American Flag at their head stormed into the Japanese camp, threatened them to leave Toledo, and forced them into cars. The mob took charge of the belongings of our countrymen and put it onto the cars, and all were taken to the outskirts of Corvallis.

Mr. Johnson, the vice-president and general manager of the Pacific Spruce Corporation took the witness stand next and made a statement advantageous to the plaintiffs, which took about an hour. He said that on the day in question, a mob intruded onto company property, carrying the Stars and Stripes at its head, so the company tried to stop them, but this resulted in the injury of three company employees. He also listed the names of the defendants as the ringleaders of the mob.

After a 10-minute break, the next witness was shipping clerk, Mr. McMurray, who made a strong statement in favor of the plaintiffs in describing the situation at the time and that a mass meeting was held in Toledo on July 11 last year. The defendants' lawyer

Green disputed the testimony, as if our countrymen left the town of their own volition. But [Collier] gave a telling reply, saying that the Japanese eviction was planned in advance, and showed the flyer used to call the meeting as evidence. Court was adjourned at 4:40 p.m. and the trial is to resume at 10 a.m., July 14.

The gallery was packed with white and Japanese observers.

The article carries a subtle nationalism throughout. Again the term "our countrymen" is used and it isn't just the flag that is carried, but "the Stars and Stripes", a symbol held before the world denoting freedom and justice. The reporter covering the trial understood how to write an effective column. How could the Stars and Stripes symbolize justice when the mob waving that flag is bent on injustice? As the reporter stated both "white and Japanese observers" were on hand to see how court officials would answer this question.

The plaintiff's attorney continued calling witnesses on the third day of the trial (Translation #5). The day was one of emotional testimony and bold court motions by the defense.

Translation by Hiroko Takada Amick and Glen-Paul Amick.

Translation #5

(See Appendix C for original Japanese text)

The Great Northern Daily News

(Taihoku Nippo)

July 15, 1926

Toledo Incident

Third Day of Trial

(From the Portland branch)

The trial resumed at 2 p.m. with Mrs. Altree, a beautiful woman, as the 1st witness. According to her testimony, before the mob rushed in on the Japanese, two white people were talking in rough language. She said that after awhile a mob of about 300 people crowded in, with one of the defendants, Owen Hart, waving the American Flag and another person shooting a pistol several times.[6]

The next witness was Ichiro Kawamoto's wife, who testified via an interpreter that she and her husband were assaulted. In the midst of this testimony she became emotional and started crying, which caused the people in the gallery to murmur to each other; she must have moved them a great deal.

The gist of her testimony was that she saw one Japanese bleeding and then seven white people forced their way into her home and beat her husband. Her bleeding husband was dragged out of the house by two Americans, while she herself took her children out of the house. Three American men and women took her laundry off of the clothesline and threw it into her face.

Testimony was next heard from Captain [William] Matthews of the *Newport News* [sic]. The gist of his testimony was that he said [he] knows the faces of the defendants and he did not see them hurt any of the Japanese.

Next came the testimony of the correspondent Lester Martin. According to his testimony, it looked like H. Germer was the leader of the mob. He saw that some company employees were bleeding from the nose. He heard someone say that they were going to expel the

Japanese by car.

Since the plaintiffs' attorney was to introduce the next witness at 3:30 p.m. and there was still some time, the defendants' lawyer, Mr. Green, spoke up and as according to the testimony so far [said that] Mrs. Schenck did not hurt any Japanese, he asked that charges against her be dismissed. As Judge Wolverton denied the motion, Mr. Green made a motion that charges against all the defendants be dismissed, which the Judge also denied.

Thereafter the witness for the defense, Harry Pritchard, took the stand and testified about the evening of July 11th at the meeting, which some 70 people attended. He said that the crowd discussed . . . the Japanese hired by the company, about the situation in the area and that the people of the area did not want them to live there, so they should leave voluntarily. Also, weapons should not be carried.

The next day they went to the company to negotiate and asked for a Japanese interpreter, but the President of the company made them angry by saying that they had to leave immediately, and if they failed to, six or so of the mob might get killed, but it would be their own fault. The court adjourned before his testimony was complete.

Today, the 15th, there is a naturalization exam at the court, so the Toledo eviction trial is in recess.

Green contended that since Mrs. Schenck wasn't present the day of the mob's activities she shouldn't be held responsible for their actions and therefore deserved to be released from the charges. This motion met with an immediate and definite negative response from Judge Wolverton. Although absent the day the mob took action against the Japanese, Mrs. Schenck was present during the mass meeting the evening before. Her presence at that assembly tied her to the conspiracy issue argued by the plaintiff.

Several reporters were impressed with the sympathetic impact Mrs. Kawamoto's passionate testimony appeared to make in the courtroom. Headlines in the *Oregon Daily Journal* on July 15 read, "Japanese Mother Sobs... Mrs. Kawamoto's earnest manner, her relation of a terrible fright given her and her breakdown while answering questions put through an interpreter stirred every spectator in the crowded court room." Although Mrs. Kawamoto's fright at having her home invaded was sincere, according to *Issei* Portlander John T. Yoneyama, he was told attorney Collier coached Mrs. Kawamoto prior to her testimony, "Just cry, whatever you are asked, just cry. Don't try to answer."[7] If their plan was to increase jury sympathy for the Japanese, their plan worked; Mrs. Kawamoto's tears stirred emotion in the courtroom.

The article's opening paragraph highlights the difficult conditions involved in both trial work and research. Owen Hart didn't carry the flag the day of the incident and no one actually fired the gun that was later thrown into Depot Slough. These inconsistencies occur often when several witnesses remember an event differently. Facts are further obscured as people revise history to place themselves in a better light. As the defense began to support their case during the third day of the trial a different story from that of the plaintiff's perspective started to emerge.[8]

As the trial continued, *The Great Northern Daily News* kept pace. An article published in July 16 detailed the drama taking place in the courtroom (Translation #6).

Translation by Hiroko Takada Amick and Glen-Paul Amick.

Translation #6
(see Appendix C for original Japanese text)
The Great Northern Daily News
[Taihoku Nippo]
July 16, 1926
Toledo Incident
[Thursday July 15th]
Court Battle heated

They dragged me out of the house with my wife.

Dean Johnson from the Pacific Spruce Corporation speaks:

A mob went into the Japanese compound and grabbed the Japanese out from their homes. Sheriff Horsfall and Deputy Daniels arrived and arrested Germer and Colvin and took them away. Horsfall took down the names of the mob. Most of them started to go away. But, Germer and Colvin came back and yelled "Come back people, the Japs have not gone out of the town yet, but they will leave this afternoon."

C.D. Johnson said to Sheriff Horsfall, "You are protecting this property. I'm giving this property over to you." Then Johnson went to his office. About forty-five minutes later he saw the mob taking the Japanese to waiting trucks. People at the platform were clapping their hands and they followed the rest of the mob.

Two Americans took Mrs. Kawamoto's laundry off the line and threw it into her face and said, "Here, you are forgetting something." In the morning Plaintiff Tamakichi Ogura spoke and in the afternoon Ichiro Kawamoto spoke.

Mr. Kawamoto understands many things. He had a contract with the mill to bring 60 workers to the company. Mr. Kawamoto testified that people were throwing stones and sticks into their compound like rain. He was forcefully taken out from his house and he was bleeding from the nose. His wife was also taken out of the house and someone took his dog away from him. He was told to get out of his house in two minutes. When he asked, "why?" the answer was, "Any reason is fine, we don't want Japanese staying here anymore." Kawamoto told them that he had a contract with the mill and that he would not go. He was told, "You leave or we are going to hang you and kill you." They pushed Mr. Kawamoto to the floor and took him and his wife from their home.

Although the riot took place the year before, readers are reminded of Kawamoto's dangerous situation and the risk he took standing up for his rights when challenged by the mob.

As the defense started presenting its case, the defendants began softening the harshness of the circumstances by asserting that the Japanese residents had misinterpreted their actions. The defense contended that: 1) although the protesters had wanted the *Issei* workers to leave Toledo, the group intended no violence, 2) that no violence had actually taken place and 3) that they went to the Japanese compound merely to explain their position (Translation #7).

Translation by Hiroko Takada Amick and Glen-Paul Amick.

Translation #7
(See Appendix C for
original Japanese text)
The Great Northern Daily News
(Taihoku Nippo)
July 17, 1926
Toledo Incident
4th day of Trial
[Friday July 16]
Defendant's Testimony
Defendant Falters
Under Cross-Examination by Plaintiff

The 4th day of the trial resumed under Judge Wolverton at 10 a.m., continuing on from the previous day, and one of the defendants, Harry Pritchard, was the first to undergo examination.

Defendant Pritchard testified that at the meeting on the evening of July 11 he advised the group not to use violence. To Attorney Collier's question as to whether anybody was agitating for the use of violence, he said no. Attorney Collier cross-examined him further, saying that it may be true that he, who advocated making every effort for a peaceful settlement, opposed the mob's violence and that he advised them not to use force; however, why did he deliberately evict the Japanese on Sunday instead of waiting until Monday or later?

Defendant Pritchard replied that the Lincoln County Protection League (LCPL) did what they could. Prior to this, the League made an appeal to the State Governor and Congressmen. He didn't know any better way than that. He believed that the Japanese themselves must have a way to cope and he waited as long as possible, but the Governor didn't provide a final solution.

Attorney Collier went for the jugular, saying "You visited the governor and asked for a settlement of this incident, but you acted with violence without waiting for the governor's solution," and Pritchard acceded that was true. It was clear the defendant's answers were inconsistent. When the plaintiff's Attorney Collier asked if he had reported to the group at the meeting on the evening of 11th that a peaceful settlement had already been reached, the defendant was quite dismayed and couldn't clearly state that he opposed the violence. He just answered that he said not to do anything until Monday. Attorney Green, who couldn't remain a mere spectator at the faltering answers of the defendant, raised an objection, but Judge Wolverton denied it flatly.

The plaintiff's Attorney Collier repeated the testimony of the plaintiff and described what happened at the eviction of the Japanese. He asked if the defendants were willing to wait until Monday before taking any action, and were opposed to the violence, then why did they in fact raid the Japanese camp as a large mob on Sunday? [Pritchard] answered that they went because they wanted to see the Japanese in person to explain the situation. But then the attorney asked if 250 people were needed for this. He answered that he didn't have an accurate count of how many people were there, but if only one person had gone, the Japanese wouldn't have taken the matter seriously. Attorney Collier sarcastically said that perhaps 75 people went to explain things to the 29 Japanese.

There were contradictions between the testimony defendant Pritchard gave today and that at the trial

> on Wednesday afternoon. In addition, he denied the testimony of the plaintiffs Ichiro Kawamoto and his wife, pretending that the mob didn't force them to leave town.

The pace of the verbal volley increased between attorney and witness as Pritchard struggled to turn the mob's actions from violent to benign.

As with any news story continuing over several days, there comes a point when the initial information behind the story needs to be repeated to allow new readers to follow current events. An editorial in *The Great Northern Daily News* provided a recap of the trial. The underlying racial tensions and violence of the mob are clearly outlined (Translation #8).

Translation by Hiroko Takada Amick and Glen-Paul Amick.

> **Translation #8**
> (See Appendix C for
> original Japanese text)
> **The Great Northern Daily News**
> **(Taihoku Nippo)**
> July 19, 1926
> **Toledo Incident**
>
> The incident in which some tens of Japanese and Korean men and women were unjustly evicted from the county by a mob in Toledo, Oregon a year ago caught the attention of both the Japanese and U.S. governments at the time. Although it was reported that the Japanese government negotiated with the U.S. government, and the U.S. government negotiated with the State Governor, we had not heard that the police arrested members of

the mob that they undertook any criminal proceedings. Nevertheless, five of the Japanese victims have brought lawsuits to federal court for compensation of damages against the six members of the mob who were deemed to be the leaders. In fact, the trial is now being held in Portland, as reported in this paper every day.

Because of the nature of the trial, there are great differences between the claims of the plaintiffs and the defendants. One side is trying to prove that they were threatened and evicted from the county, while the other is attempting to prove that it was not an eviction, and the Orientals left of their own free will. The verdict will depend on the evidence, so I dare not try to guess what the verdict will be, but seek to share my observations about the testimony from both sides to date, insofar as they are consistent with each other.

What has been acknowledged by both sides as true, without witnesses on either side contesting the other's statement is as follows:

As it was not desired by the Toledo residents that Orientals be hired by the Pacific Spruce Corporation, the residents sought a meeting with the governor or the Japanese consul, stated their opinion that the Orientals should not be hired, and wrote to a member of the upper house asking for assistance. A mass meeting was held to discuss how to make the Orientals leave and then acted on it. A large crowd rushed over to property of the corporation with the American flag at their head, and some were yelling to beat up the Japs while fighting on company property with its workers, inflicting bloodshed. Then they swooped down to the Japanese residential area and straight away loaded the cars they had hired with the Orientals and their belongings, drove them outside the county border and dropped them off there.

— (P.2) —

The above is a summation of the points that both sides agree upon, and from this we learned that the Toledo residents fiercely despised the coming of the Orientals.

Although it may make the capitalists happy to send Orientals to places where they are so unpopular, it is unwise. If the Japanese went to such an area without knowing how poorly they would be received, the capitalists or someone must have misled them. It was learned afterwards that not enough attention had been given to this matter since the Japanese Consulate had heard about this from workers prior to the incident.

Even though they may think that they were at the end of their rope, when the local people took the action of rushing together in a large crowd to evict them, nonetheless, all the steps had not yet been exhausted.

If the capitalist thinks it through, it is reasonable for the Orientals to team up with the white workers against the capitalist, for it is in their interest of self-protection. However, we didn't know that on the contrary that when the Oriental worker stands with the capitalist against the white worker, that the white worker would be so angry, extending at times to violence.

In Washington State the year before the last, Japanese who worked for the railroad got caught between the workers and the capitalist, and were put in a difficult position. When there is a dispute between the workers and the capitalist, in principle, workers should stand with their fellow workers.

The writer takes an interesting stand in his editorial, more of an economic than a racial perspective. Not only does he acknowledge that government on both sides failed to take the mounting crisis seriously, but his overall point that cooperation is in the best interest of all workers, strikes an oddly resonant chord with the original intent of the LCPL. The "capitalists," in his opinion, is The Pacific Spruce Corporation, the "white workers" represent the protestors. In an odd way, the reporter agrees with the protesters' intent, though not with their methods. Although his argument has merit, the Toledo protesters were not mill workers and so were not of the same economic rank as the *Issei*. This is an important distinction.

Defense testimony given on July 19 contradicted much of the plaintiff's earlier testimony. As the trial continued, Collier cross-examined the Toledo defendants, picking apart the weaker areas of their testimony (Translation #9).

Translation by Hiroko Takada Amick and Glen-Paul Amick.

Translation #9

(See Appendix C for original Japanese text)

The Great Northern Daily News (Taihoku Nippo)

July 20, 1926

Portland July 19th [Monday]

Toledo Incident

5th Day of the Trial

The trial of the Toledo Incident continued, resuming at 2 p.m. today under Judge Wolverton. The gallery was packed with Japanese and white people.

As a witness for the defense, A. Jacobson, who lost one arm working for the Spruce Corporation, took the witness stand and denied the plaintiff's claims, saying that he joined the gathering, but the crowd did not use violence. The plaintiff's attorney, Mr. Collier directed a question to Jacobson as to whether the crowd said anything to the Japanese. Jacobson replied that the crowd didn't say anything, but the white people and the Japanese were conversing, and that since the Japanese left Toledo, they were going to sue the Pacific Spruce Corporation. The plaintiff's attorney in turn, asked who the white and Japanese people were who were conversing. [Jacobson] evaded the question by saying he didn't know because he was 30 feet away from them. Then it was pointed out that he has lived in Toledo for quite a long time and yet he didn't know who was standing just 30 feet away, but he pretended not to know and withdrew from the stand.

Next came the testimony of G.W. Hall, a Toledo weekly paper reporter. He spoke for the defense and said that he went to the site after 3 p.m., which was after the incident occurred, but he didn't hear anything about evicting the Japanese and claimed that he had absolutely nothing to do with the incident. When the plaintiff's attorney Collier stuck the red flyer used for the mass meeting in front of his face and asked who requested him to print it, he gave an ambiguous reply, saying that he was a reporter, and didn't know who did, but maybe his brother printed it.

According to the report from the state governor, when Secretary Delzell went on a business trip to Toledo after the incident occurred, a meeting was held at the home of Mr. Schenck to discuss what to do. Mr. Schenck is thought to have been an instigator of the incident. The plaintiff's attorney asked whether [Hall] was there, and he evaded the question saying with feigned innocence that he attended as a newspaper reporter. But in answer to close questioning by the plaintiff's attorney, he confessed that he is a member of the Toledo Citizens Protection League.

— (P.2) —

After his testimony came to a close, the next witness, R.C. Hart, a brother of Owen Hart, one of the defendants, and who is said to have taken our fellow Japanese to Corvallis, took the stand. He testified that he was on the baseball playground when the incident occurred and didn't know how things happened in the incident; however, after the incident, Japanese were in town and he took them to Corvallis by car. The plaintiff's attorney cross-examined him, asking who asked him to take them by car. He answered the townspeople asked him, so he did. When asked if the mob asked him to do so, he replied no, and testified that he carried them by car but he didn't receive any money.

Then the trial moved on to the testimony of Owen Hart. The defendant testified with quite a frivolous attitude and an asinine smile on his face that he fought with a company guard and got a black eye, so he hit the company guard back; however, the company guard didn't shake hands afterwards. As to a more serious point of this incident, which was breaking down the door of a Japanese house, he gave himself away saying that since the door to the Japanese house was closed, he entered through the window and opened the door. Next, C. Bredstead took the witness stand and denied the claims made by the plaintiff. He stated that the Japanese left of their own free will. The Court was adjourned at 4:30 and the trial continues tomorrow.

The reporter's presentation of witness attitude and response makes one wonder why these witnesses weren't cited for contempt of court, or obstruction, or something that would show that the court recognized some of the witnesses weren't being direct in their answers.

As the sixth day of the trial continued, the defense team presented both character and eye witnesses. *The Great Northern Daily News* continued its coverage (Translation #10):

Translation by Hiroko Takada Amick and Glen-Paul Amick.

Translation #10
(See Appendix C for
original Japanese text)
The Great Northern Daily News
(Taihoku Nippo)
July 21, 1926

Toledo Incident
6th Day of Trial. (July 20, 1926)
(From the Portland Branch)

The first person the defense attorney called to the witness stand on Tuesday was the pastor, C. Morris of Wending, who was preaching at the Methodist Church in July last year, as well as being an organizer of the Toledo Chamber of Commerce. The defense attorney asked, "While you were working for the Chamber of Commerce, did the officers do anything about the Japanese workers?" However, the attorney for the plaintiff objected, so the witness could not reply.

P.I. Macintyre [sic], who took two Japanese from Toledo to Corvallis, testified that he took them without having been asked by anybody to do so and that he didn't receive any money for it. The wife of the undertaker and furniture storeowner, Mrs. Ethel Bateman was one of the associate officers of the Lincoln County Protection League and is thought to have testified on behalf of the defendant, Mrs. Schenck.

According to Mrs. Bateman, she was at Mrs. Schenck's house from 2 to 4 p.m. on the Sunday in question [when the incident occurred] along with other men and women, and they discussed a plan to visit the governor or Congressman McNary to discuss the Japanese workers.

. . . An important witness presented by the defense on Tuesday was Arthur E. Marvin, a Toledo contractor. He said that he had witnessed the riot in its entirety that afternoon on July 12th last year. He first spoke of a big crowd breaking through the company entrance and then rushing over to the Japanese residences. Under questioning from the defense attorney, he further testified that there was no violence and the Japanese saw how things were and left of their own accord.

In brief, he testified as follows . . . "After the aforementioned dispute, the authorities of the company didn't make any attempt to protest, and we went to where the Japanese were living. The Japs were inside their homes. One of them came out of a house and asked why so many people were crowding around. So we explained that we didn't want them here in Toledo. So, the Japanese replied, 'We will leave.' And then he knocked on the other doors and informed the other Japanese of this."

A question and answer session then ensued between the witness and the defense attorney.

"Were any Japanese houses, doors or windows

pushed open?"

"No."

"Were any doors or windows broken?"

"No."

"Were any Japanese treated roughly?"

"No."

"Did any Japanese mingle in the group afterwards?"

"Yes."

"Did you see any Japanese with blood or their clothes or face?"

"No."

"Were any Japanese harassed or threatened in town?"

"No."

Mrs. Bateman's testimony lent support for Mrs. Schenck (who still hoped to separate herself from the actions of the mob) but it was Arthur E. Marvin who was considered the strongest witness for the defense. Speaking clearly and quickly, he provided considerable detail of the protesters' actions when they reached the *Issei* quarters.[9]

The following day, July 21, 1926, two important defense witnesses took the stand: W.S. Colvin and Rosemary Schenck. As Attorney Collier began questioning Colvin, Collier first pointed out that foreman Kawamoto failed to come out of his house on July 12, 1925 because of fright after witnessing several fights between the Toledo crowd and the deputies of the mill. Colvin responded with the statement that the "head man" had had nothing to fear, "Our purpose in going to the Japanese quarters was to plead with the Japs and to show them they were taking the places of white men in their work." Colvin added, "I know they are a sensible people and we wanted to tell them the true circumstances of the situation."[10] Colvin appeared to believe that the Pacific Spruce Corporation misrepresented themselves to the Japanese they brought in to work the green-chain, otherwise why would the Japanese need to have the "true circumstances" explained to them?

Collier continued to question Colvin, "Would you have shown the Japs more consideration than you did those who were guarding the property of the man who keeps your town alive?" Colvin snapped back that C.D. Johnson was "the very man who brought the Japs in to kill our town." Moving on to another question, Collier asked about Colvin's flag carried by the Toledo mob, "This emblem of liberty waved while you people were beating up three or four guards?" Colvin replied, "If the guards had allowed the Japanese interpreter to come out and talk to a delegation from the crowd, there would have been no blows struck and all trouble would have been averted."[11] Colvin's statements, as those of other defense witnesses, were designed to turn the blame from themselves on to the one they considered to be the true troublemaker: the Pacific Spruce Corporation.

Mrs. Schenck took the stand after William Colvin. She went into detail about her quest to get various officials' support blocking the Japanese from coming to Toledo. The defense had several of Mrs. Schenck's telegrams they wanted to enter into evidence on their behalf, but attorneys Thompson and Collier blocked most of them. Judge Wolverton did allow one set of telegrams to be admitted. Within this group of telegrams was a communication from Mrs. Schenck to acting Secretary of Labor, Robert Carl White, in Washington D. C.:

> The Pacific Spruce Corporation at Toledo employed about 35 coolies to work in its sawmill. Citizens of the county protested, and before the Japanese actually had begun work they were taken out

> of the county and taken to the depot at Corvallis, Oregon. There is no labor trouble at this time, and none is contemplated. —ROSEMARY SCHENCK[12]

The apparent purpose of submitting Mrs. Schenck's telegram into evidence was to demonstrate that the Lincoln County Protective League did everything in its power to prevent the Japanese from coming to Toledo in the first place and later to get the *Issei* out of the county peacefully. But the strategy backfired. The plaintiff's lawyers used the telegram to show that the Japanese did not leave voluntarily, but were "taken out of the county" and "taken to the depot" in Corvallis.

Rosemary's husband, George Schenck was also on the witness stand that afternoon. During his cross-examination of Schenck, Collier attempted to address one of the biggest questions of the trial—why did City Marshal George Schenck fail to provide protection for the Japanese residents? Schenck did not provide a satisfactory justification for his conduct, and to his frustration, embarrassed himself—much to the amusement of the entire court (Translation #11). Schenck had little to say that would exonerate himself or his actions.

Translation by Hiroko Takada Amick and Glen-Paul Amick.

Translation #11

(See Appendix M for original Japanese text)

The Great Northern Daily News

July 22, 1926 [Wednesday, July 21st]

Toledo Incident

7th Day of Trial

(Portland Branch Report)

Last Wednesday, a scene took place that caused everyone in the gallery to burst into laughter in spite of themselves. The person who caused the unexpected explosion of laughter in the solemn courtroom was none other than Mr. Schenck, the Toledo police chief.

He was invited by the attorney for the defense, Mr. Green to take the witness stand midway through the afternoon session. After testifying that he didn't know anything about the assaults at all, he was cross-examined by the plaintiff's attorney Mr. Collier for over thirty minutes about various questions.

Mr. Collier directed sharp questions, such as that while it was his job to maintain public order as the chief of police, he testified that he stayed at home despite the knowledge of his deputies going to the scene of a potential riot, thus leaving the job of maintaining order to the deputies, so does he think he can escape the duty he was getting paid for?

Mr. Schenck was dismayed and not knowing what to reply to that question, just wiped the sweat from his face. Seeing this, defense attorney Mr. Green, came to his rescue saying, "your honor, such a question has little relevance to the incident; please stop this." The judge replied, "the police chief is in charge of maintaining public order, so it is reasonable that these questions should be broadly asked." Accordingly, Mr. Collier interrogated him the more fiercely. Then, Mr. Green stood up again and said, "it is not fair for you to badger my witness like this;" however, picking up the usage of badger, Mr. Collier stood up and said "I am not badgering him." Then Mr. Schenck stood up and countered, "please don't say things to offend me," and in reply to this Mr. Collier retorted, "I don't recall saying anything offensive about you."

"You said that I am a badger," the police chief said angrily. As Mr. Collier pointed out to him, "it was your attorney who said that," the whole court broke into laughter. The English term badger can mean to harass, or as a noun, the animal badger.

Next, A.R. Richardson, a contractor of some 60 years of age, took the witness stand and testified in response to the defense attorney's questions that the Toledo crowd had been peaceful. The riot on that day only came about when the crowd tried to enter company property and the company personnel rebuffed them. When they went to the Japanese residential compound, there was no discord. He also testified that if the plaintiff Mr. Ogura had known the Toledo residents' feelings about Japanese, he would not have come to Toledo. He then testified that (Ogura) said that if he had the money, he would leave, which is why the hat was passed, raising $140 or so, which was given to the Japanese.

The conclusion of the trial is finally approaching. After the trial was adjourned yesterday, as the attorney for the plaintiff, Mr. Green, indicated his cross-examination of witnesses would finish around noon on Thursday, the closing arguments will take place shortly thereafter and then the judge's instructions to the jury and finally the jurors will deliberate the matter.

Following the testimony of Chief of Police Schenck, defendant W. S. Colvin took the stand and testified in agreement that there was no violence at all. Mrs. Schenck and Peter Townsend also testified.

Schenck's folly on the stand didn't help the defendants' case, and Richardson's statement that the Toledo group collected one hundred forty dollars for the Japanese residents is at odds with the *Issei* account that only thirty dollars and thirty-six cents was raised.

The *Oregon Daily Journal* reported Schenck's cross-examination in more detail: Mr. Schenck told Attorney Collier that he knew little of what was being done by the Lincoln County Protective League before the day of the riot. He testified so despite the fact that his wife was the Secretary of that organization. He declared that he knew nothing of the mass meeting held July 11th or that the group was planning to visit the Japanese homes the following day. Schenck admitted that he had warned Mrs. Kawamoto and the other *Issei* with her on Saturday afternoon, telling them to "go back to Tokio [sic] on the mill property."

Schenck's attempt at disassociating himself from the actions of the LCPL didn't work. His duty as City Marshal was to protect all the people within his town. George Schenck went for a drive in the country Saturday evening, July 11th. Attorney Collier asked him about this trip, "What business did you have out in the country?

Schenck replied, "out on pleasure."

Collier then asked, "and yet you knew the temper of the people was such that afternoon as to warn the Japs?"

"I found it convenient to take a little ride," Schenck answered.

"Yes, yes," Collier said. "Just a little ride in the fresh air."[13]

As closing arguments in the trial got underway on Thursday afternoon, July 22, two main issues were discussed: whether the Japanese left town voluntarily on the afternoon of July 12, 1925 or whether they were driven out by a conspiring, angry mob. *Issei* attorneys John Collier and Lair Thompson presented the plaintiffs' argument. Collier began by saying:

> It is the contention of the Japanese plaintiffs that they were attacked in their homes at the Pacific Spruce Corporation's property by an unreasoning and rough crowd of Toledo citizens who, after beating and kicking some of them, forced them to leave town.

The charge of conspiracy, Collier said, was the important point for the jury to consider. This he declared was the great offense. And, according to the theory he told to the jury, every member of the so-called mob was responsible for the actions of all other members.

The conspiracy theory stems from Thompson and Collier's argument that although the mob acted as one body, it was the individuals of that body that determined the action taken, thus the individuals conspired together: first in the meeting on July 11, 1925, when citizens concerned about the Japanese coming to Toledo met together to decide what action to take and then the following day when they banded together to carry out their plan.

Thompson's argument for the plaintiff featured attacks on the mass meeting held by Toledo townspeople the night before the deportation episode in which the crowd was told, "we have exhausted every peaceful means." He also criticized the Toledo City Marshal George Schenck by saying that Schenck was, "watching Rome burn while he fiddled."[14]

However, defense attorneys Turner, Krause and B. A. Green held that it wasn't the individuals who had caused the trouble but rather Pacific Spruce Corporation. They reminded the jury of their interpretation of the riot:

> Turner declared the Toledo community was like any other in the state and the people were no different from the average residents of a small town. They were good citizens and peaceful, he said.
>
> At the door of the Pacific Spruce Corporation he laid the responsibility for the origin of the trouble. The community had worked in harmony with the company, he said, until the Japanese were brought in. This, the people felt, meant that many of the white residents of the town would be replaced by Orientals.
>
> They were distressed, he declared, and explained their feelings to the Japanese. There was no rough treatment

> shown the Orientals, according to the attorney, and they left town voluntarily when the situation was shown them.[15]

Had the corporation, Turner argued, listened to the Toledo citizens concerned about losing their livelihoods there wouldn't have been any trouble with the Japanese. In this view, culpability lay with Pacific Spruce Corporation, not the mob.

After both sides had presented their arguments, the court adjourned for the day.

The next day, Friday, July 23, saw the largest public turnout of the nine-day trial. Black, Japanese and Chinese were all represented in the courtroom. Attorney Collier took up most of the morning with his closing argument, "The jury system is on trial in this case," he informed the jurors. "If the United States-Japanese treaty is to be regarded as being but a scrap of paper, that is for you to say. This is a case of mob violence. And in all parts of this country and other countries, people are waiting to hear what this jury does today."[16] Collier urged the jurors to try the case based on the testimony and the evidence and not allow racial differences to enter into their considerations. He once again reminded the jury that Japanese residents were granted protection under the law. Because of this the Japanese had the right to live and work in the United States without fear of violence.

That same day, *The Oregon Daily Journal* ran the following article:

> ...Judge Wolverton instructed the jurors to disregard racial differences or prejudice, defined the meaning of "conspiracy," and directed that if conspiracy were found proven, all conspirators should be held equally responsible and directed that damages suffered by the Pacific Spruce Corporation in the mob attack against the Japanese at Toledo should be disregarded.[17]

Judge Wolverton continued with a lengthy and detailed

instruction to the jury which took almost an hour to read. He defined conspiracy "as the operation of two or more persons to accomplish an unlawful act," adding, "it is unlawful to induce Japanese to abandon their homes and jobs and unlawful to deport them." Wolverton went on to say that when "a conspiracy exists, whatever any conspirator does is binding upon all the conspirators."[18] Following his remarks the jury went into deliberation at 2:35 p.m.

Two hours and twenty minutes later the jury reached a verdict.

NOTES

[1]"Case L9713," National Archives-Pacific AK Region, Seattle, Washington.

[2]"Unions to Aid Toledo Defense" *Lincoln County Leader*, 8 Oct 1925.

[3]"Big Mass Meeting Adopts Resolution Opposing Jap Labor", *Lincoln County Leader*, 7 May 1925.

[4]"Mob Attack on Colony Described," *Oregon Daily Journal,* 13 July 1926.

[5]"Figures in Japanese-Toledo Fight," *Oregon Daily Journal,* 14 July 1926.

[6]This report is incorrect. Owen Hart did not carry the flag and there were no shots fired.

[7]Ito, Kazuo, *Issei: A history of Japanese Immigrants in North America.* S. Nakamura, J. Gerard (Seattle, Washington 1973) 215.

[8]"Japanese Suits Draw Interest of Two Nations," *Oregon Daily Journal,* 18 July 1926.

[9]"Blames Boy for Toledo Racial Row," *Oregon Daily Journal*, 20 July 1926.

[10]"Argument in Toledo Case is Underway," *Oregon Daily Journal,* 22 July 1926.

[11]"Argument in Toledo," *Journal.*

[12]"Chief Puts Laugh in Gloomy Trial," *Oregon Daily Journal*, 21 July 1926.

[13]"Chief Puts Laugh," *Journal*.

[14]"Argument in Toledo," *Journal*.

[15]"Argument in Toledo," *Journal*.

[16]"Finale at Hand in Toledo Case," *Oregon Daily Journal.* 23 July 1926.

[17]"Finale at Hand," *Journal*.

[18]"Toledo People Must Pay Damages to Ousted Japanese," *Lincoln County Leader* 29 July 1926.

Chapter 7: The Judgment

The Judgment

The decision came at the end of the federal court day as Judge Wolverton was about to instruct the Jury to bring in a sealed verdict if they reached a decision after-hours. Because it was late in the afternoon, the twelve man jury announced their decision to an almost empty courtroom.[1] Howard P. Boardman, the jury foreman, stood up and read the decision.

National Archives-Pacific AK Region, Seattle, WA.

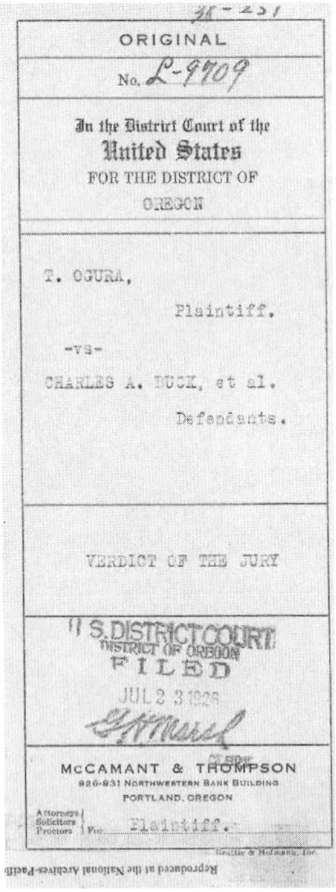
ORIGINAL

No. L-9709

In the District Court of the United States FOR THE DISTRICT OF OREGON

T. OGURA,
Plaintiff.
-vs-
CHARLES A. BUCK, et al.
Defendants.

VERDICT OF THE JURY

U.S. DISTRICT COURT
DISTRICT OF OREGON
FILED
JUL 23 1926

McCAMANT & THOMPSON
926-931 NORTHWESTERN BANK BUILDING
PORTLAND, OREGON
Attorneys / Solicitors / Proctors for Plaintiff.

Reproduced at the National Archives-Pacific

38. Although charges were dropped against Buck, his name went through the court process as can be seen on this verdict filing.

> We the jury, duly impaneled in the above entitled court and cause find for the plaintiff in the sum of twenty five hundred (2500) dollars, and against the defendants, W.S. Colvin, H.T. Pritchard, Frank Sturdevant, Owen Hart, Rosemary Schenck and George R. Schenck.[2]

As the decision was announced, defense attorney Green asked that the jury be polled. Each of the twelve jurors stood and affirmed the verdict. Green then declared that his clients would be unable to pay any damages that might be imposed, "They cannot even meet the attorney's fees in such a suit."[3] Green further charged that the lawsuit was a deliberate attempt by the Pacific Spruce Corporation to "break these people" and force them to leave their community.[4]

Issei attorney W. Lair Thompson commented to reporters that:

> The verdict is a victory for law and order. It will be welcomed by law-abiding citizens everywhere. It is a tribute to the courage and sound common sense of American juries. Had the Japanese been employed in a place of established industry, there would have been no trouble. It is a known fact that every sizable sawmill in the northwest is compelled to man the green-chain with foreigners or negroes, because white men won't do that work. This was all the Pacific Spruce Corporation did and their actions would not have been questioned, except that the people were not familiar with the sawmill business.[5]

Following Thompson's announcement he officially filed the "Verdict of the Jury" (Photograph 38) with the district court.

The successful outcome of the lawsuit meant much more to the Oregon Japanese Association than just recovering damages. *Issei* regarded the trial as a test to see whether or not they could live and work in America undisturbed.[6] The trial confirmed this right. The case established for the first time in a federal civil suit that legal aliens living in the United States had civil rights, which could not be violated by the will of local populations without possible consequences.[7] In attorney Collier's opinion, if the Toledo defendants had won the case, other communities throughout the United States would have been encouraged to commit similar acts of wrong doing.[8]

With legal fees mounting and four similar civil suits in line for trial, the defendants realized they were losing financial control of their lives. It was then decided to negotiate an out-of-court settlement. With Attorney Green acting on their behalf, a settlement was reached on October 1, 1926 with details of the settlement printed in *The Great Northern Daily News*.

Translation by Hiroko Takada Amick and Glen-Paul Amick.

Translation #12

(See Appendix C for original Japanese article)

The Great Northern Daily News (Taihoku Nippo)

October 1st, 1926

Toledo Anti-Japanese Incident Defendants Pay Damages

They obey the verdict and promise not to oust Japanese in the future. Other suits withdrawn

The lawsuit brought by our compatriot for compensation of damages of $130,000 against Mr. and Mrs. Schenck et al. was won by the plaintiff under the fair judgment of the late Judge Wolverton, and the defendants were ordered to pay $2,500 as compensation. Since the trial consumed most of the defendants' assets and they are in a state of bankruptcy, their attorney, Mr. Green, sought goodwill from the plaintiff's attorney Thompson after the verdict was handed down. As a result of the deliberations, the Japanese side invoked the conditions that the defendants consent to the verdict and pay damages of $2,500, as well as that they do not evict or protest against the Japanese coming to work. The defendants accepted this, and the incident was settled at a meeting in the office of attorney Thompson yesterday afternoon. The above matter was agreed by Mr. Tamayoshi [Tamakichi] Ogura, and at the same time, other matters, relating to Mrs. Kawamoto, Mr. Tsubokawa and the late Mr. Mitsuya [Mitani] were withdrawn in recognition of the sincerity of the defendants.

The defendants were required to pay court costs, but more important to the *Issei*, the defendants were obliged to promise that there would be no hostile acts against any *Issei* who might return to work in Toledo. None ever did.

Due to Judge Wolverton's untimely death on September 21, 1926 Federal Judge Robert S. Bean was assigned to the case. On Saturday, October 2, he signed the order dismissing the four untried suits. Fred Ross from the Farm-Labor Legal Bureau was assigned trustee to coordinate the collection and to disperse the settlement money.[9]

The total cost to the Toledo defendants is not known since documents pertaining to the out of court settlement were not made public. Without a public record for reference, the amount can only be estimated. Court records indicate that in addition to the twenty five hundred dollar settlement there were also court costs totaling six hundred ninety dollars and forty cents. This brought the total amount paid to the *Issei* to three thousand one hundred ninety dollars and forty cents. Other court related costs added significantly to the total that was eventually paid. Mr. John T. Yoneyama, who participated in an oral history that was published in Kazuo Ito's classic book, *Issei: A History of Japanese Immigrants in North America,* said the defendants had to come up with a total of sixty-five hundred dollars.[10]

On October 14, 1926 the *Lincoln County Leader* printed an article detailing compensation payments that had been made to that point:

> The Leader has heard many requests as to just how much money the settling of the Japanese cases has cost the Lincoln County citizens who were defendants in the case. Up to the present time only three defendants have contributed to the case. These are Mr. and Mrs. Schenck, W.S. Colvin and several Lincoln County citizens who were not connected with the case. When the settlement was made it took exactly $4868.59 to cover the costs of

court and the amount turned to the Japanese. This sum was raised by the following people:

George Schenck	$2,000
Rosemary Schenck	$2,000
W.S. Colvin	$600
Fred Ross—trustee	
(donated by Lincoln County Citizens)	$268
Total	$4,868[11]

All of the defendants felt repercussions from this settlement for years to come.

Pritchard lost his clothing store and apparently left town without paying any portion of the settlement. The Schenck's sold a significant part of their Toledo properties to finance the bulk of the settlement fees.[12] The Colvins were able to pay their portion of the settlement and stay in business in Toledo for a few more years. On May 19, 1927 Owen Hart paid three hundred and fifty dollars to Fred Ross to settle his portion of the Ogura judgment. He continued to make payments for a number of years to pay off his debt accrued from the out-of-court settlement.[13]

Unfortunately for Frank Sturdevant, his portion of the Ogura settlement resulted in the courthouse auction of his property on July 23, 1927 by U.S. Marshal Clarence R. Hotchkiss:

> I did sell all the right, title and interest which . . .Frank Sturdevant had on the date of the Judgment for his property. . . for the sum of three hundred dollars. . .being the highest and best sum bid. The estimated value was three thousand dollars.[14]

Fred Ross, from the Farm-Labor Legal Bureau, was the only bidder.

Jackie Robeson was just seven years old when her parents moved to Toledo in 1927. She lived in the same neighborhood as the Schencks, Colvins and Sturdevants. While growing up she played and attended school with Schenck and Colvin children. She recalled that the Sturdevant house sat empty for a long time after she moved to Toledo. As a child she played in the empty house and was impressed with all the dishes stacked in the dining room cabinet.

> That was something nobody talked about in Toledo. It was just something that you didn't mention. We were told as kids not to mention that to anybody. Of course the Colvin and Schencks may have talked about it among themselves. We knew that they were bitter about it from their attitude and little remarks that were made. But they never talked about it in front of me. I remember the Colvins were very bitter about the lawsuit because they lost so much.[15]

For the defendants who remained in Toledo, there would have been reminders of what they had lost and what their choices had cost them.

Owen Hart was living with his parents when his widowed sister Margaret (Hart) Sturdevant and her daughter Patricia (Sturdevant) Dye came to live with them in 1923. Patricia remembers the family reaction to the Toledo deportation. "It was considered unfortunate and was not discussed in the family. My grandparents considered that it was something Owen did when he was young and didn't know any better and that was the end of it."[16] That she can remember the family's response so clearly indicates how deeply affected the family was by the event and trial.

From a judicial perspective the legal implications of this lawsuit were not as far-reaching as they could have been had the case gone on to the appellate court. This is because a case that is appealed will generally have a written opinion that is published and placed in law libraries throughout the country. Lawyers use these opinions to support cases that they are working on. Thus a precedent set in appellate court has a far greater impact than a decision by a jury from the federal trial court.

Even though the legal implications were not as far-reaching as they might have been, for a time the decision did provide a deterrent for similar civil rights violations. The case gave *Issei* and other minorities a small step forward in their fight for civil liberties.[17]

Celeste Mathews, Events Coordinator for the City of Toledo, conducted an oral interview with retired Toledo barber Harry Schick in October 2004. During that interview, the Japanese deportation story came up in the conversation:

CM: There's a fellow that's writing a whole history of that incident. He's gone back to all the newspaper accounts because it was covered in the newspapers around the state. It was a regional story. And this trial took place in Portland. And he's finally...winnowed it down to the true facts of the case. Because there are a lot of rumors about the Tokyo Incident.

HS: Oh, yeah.

CM: What was the generally accepted version when you were aware if it?

HS: Well, I really wasn't aware of it until I got here 'cause I came after it was all over with. But a lot of the guys, they were really disgusted with the whole situation, the way it went down.

CM: In what way?

HS: Well, they thought it could have been handled a little different 'cause they. . .I don't know. A lot of the guys thought they kind of pushed too much. Some of them thought that they should have done more to get the Japanese out of here But a lot of them were saying, "Well, the people didn't want to work, some of them didn't want to work and they had to have somebody to do the work."

CM: Right. So they understood the mill's position in bringing them in?

HS: Yeah.

CM: Yeah. Well, the guys that worked down there must have known how much of a problem it was to keep fellows on the green-chain.

HS: Yeah, that's right.

CM: And that's why they were brought.

HS: Now, that's true.

CM: So, it wasn't actually the mill workers who got all upset about it. It was the townspeople.

HS: It was the townspeople more. I shouldn't say who it was.

CM: We know who it was! The sheriff's wife, for one.

HS: Yeah. So was Owen Hart.

CM: Owen Hart actually, it turns out, that he was playing a baseball game down there and the mob went by, and he just kind of joined in.

HS: Yeah.

CM: It wasn't a premeditated thing, it didn't seem like.

HS: Yeah. But I think he just got involved in it without realizing what he was getting into.

CM: Right. And he paid for it.

HS: Yeah, he did. Yeah, he did, he paid for it. He regretted it.

CM: So, later, after the whole thing was over and ten years or fifteen years later, did people try to avoid talking about it or did they just say, that's over and it's unfortunate. Or what did they say?

HS: Well, most people, I know when they came in the barbershop, they didn't talk very much about it anymore. After a while it kind of died down. And they wouldn't talk about it. If I'd say something about it, well they'd change the subject.

CM: Oh, would they?

HS: Yeah

CM: So, it was kind of a general feeling that we don't want to think about it anymore.

HS: Yeah.

CM: It's over. We can't change what happened.

HS: That's right

CM: Let's go on.

HS: Yeah. That's true. Yeah.

CM: So, do you think minorities were more or less accepted in the town later?

HS: Well, I think they were, really. I mean, I don't know just what I should say about that because I wasn't here and there wasn't any of them here when I came. They all left.

CM: Right.

HS: So, they were a kind of back history, I guess you would say, or something.

CM: So, pulling on the green-chain remained a problem?

HS: Yeah.

CM: ...for the mill. For years to come?

HS: Yeah, Oh, yeah. That's for sure.[18]

Mr. Schick's recollection shows that although many years have passed since the riot and the trial, the discomfort of the memories remain. The citizens of Toledo were not the only ones who remembered the riot and the trial. Recently the author interviewed Homer and Miki Yasui in the lobby of the Oregon Historical Society in downtown Portland. At that time Homer shared the following childhood memory of his father, Masuo Yasui:

When my father was still alive, we used to drive up to

> Seattle on Hwy. 99. Highway 5 was not built at that time. Whenever we passed the little town of Toledo, Washington he would get visibly upset. At first I did not understand it. He told me, "Well, you know Homer, way back when, in about 1925, the Japanese were driven out of the town of Toledo." At that time, it did not make any sense to me, because as far as I knew, we never stopped in this Washington town to see if there was a sawmill there. It didn't seem like there was anything there—until many years later I found out that he was referring to Toledo, Oregon.
>
> I know now that whenever we went by Toledo, Washington, it rang a bell in his head and he remembered Toledo, Oregon. That made him mad.[19]

Yasui's recollection, and those of others found in this book, leave no doubt that almost eighty years later the Toledo Incident remains a painful memory for some.

Minority groups continued to struggle for equality in the United States after 1926 as subsequent events across the nation were changing our society in small ways. The verdict of the Japanese-Toledo lawsuit most probably caused communities outside of Toledo to consider how they handled minority relations. While this one case didn't solve the country's problems it was undoubtedly a small step forward for minority civil rights in America.

NOTES

[1]"Japanese Wins Sum of $2500 Damages," *Oregon Daily Journal*, 24, July 1926.

[2]"Case L9709," National Archives-Pacific AK Region. Seattle, Washington.

[3]"Japanese Wins Sum of $2500," *Journal*.

[4]"Japanese Wins Sum of $2500," *Journal*.

[5]"$2500 Awarded T. Ogura," *Morning Oregonian*, 24 July 1926.

[6]"$2500 Awarded," *Morning Oregonian*.

[7]"Japanese Winning Freedom to Work," *New York Times*, 8 Aug. 1926.

[8]"Oriental Wins Toledo Action," *Oregon Statesman*, 24 July 1926.

[9]"Case L9709," National Archives.

[10]Ito, Kazuo, *Issei: A History of Japanese Immigrants in North America*, S. Nakamura, J. Gerard (Seattle, Washington 1973) 215.

[11]"Japanese Suits Have Cost Three Defendants Upwards of $5,000," *Lincoln County Leader*, 14 Oct. 1926.

[12]Lincoln County deed files. Lincoln County Court House, Newport, Oregon.

[13]Mr. and Mrs. Larry Hart, interview by author, recorded interview, Toledo, Oregon, May 21, 2004.

[14]Case L9709, National Archives.

[15]Mrs. Jackie Robeson, interview by author, recorded interview, Toledo, Oregon, June 20, 2004.

[16]Patricia Sturdevant Dye, interview by author, written notes, Toledo, Oregon, September 1, 2004.

[17]Tim Willis, interview by author, recorded interview, Corvallis, Oregon, May 18, 2004.

[18]Harry Schick, interview by Celeste Mathews at Harry's home in Toledo, Oregon, October 2004.

[19]Homer Yasui, interview by author, written notes, Portland, Oregon, April 15, 2004.

Appendix A

1884-1924: Japanese Immigration to the United States

Between 1884 and 1924 close to three hundred thousand Japanese immigrated to the United States. Many came seeking jobs which paid considerably more than in Japan. For instance in 1900 an unskilled worker earned about two cents per hour in Japan. That same unskilled worker could earn around seventeen cents per hour in the U.S..[1] Many of these immigrants returned to Japan. Those who stayed were known as *Issei,* the first generation.

Until about 1910 most Japanese immigrants were single men, many of whom planned to return to Japan after three to five years, to live an economically improved life with their savings.[2] Although up to twenty-five percent did return to Japan, many more abandoned their plans and chose to adopt the United States as their home.[3] Of the *Issei* immigrants coming to the United States, only a few thousand settled in Oregon. The largest Japanese resident populations were located in California and Washington.[4]

For over twenty-five years, Japanese immigrants were primarily men. To turn around this "bachelor society," the Japanese government began encouraging Japanese women to emigrate to the U.S.. In response to this, many Japanese women came to the United States as wives of *Issei* men, either as picture brides or with their husbands, and the 1910s became a time of significant Japanese settlement in America.[5]

The vast majority of *Issei* who decided to stay in the United States became American in spirit, deed and dress, although discriminatory law barred them from citizenship until 1952.[6] Nationalization belonged to the second generation Japanese American children. Like all children born in the United States they were American citizens.

Japanese Association Oregon
Founded 1911

The late Professor Yuji Ichioka (renowned UCLA historian), said that the most important organization for the Japanese immigrant generation in the United States was the Japanese association.[7]

In 1908 the Japanese Association of America was first established in San Francisco, replacing the United Japanese Deliberative Council of America. In 1911 the Japanese Association of Oregon was organized in Portland with chapter associations in Idaho and Wyoming. By 1923 the Oregon central association had a total of ten-affiliated chapters.[8]

What made this system special was that the Japanese government delegated limited bureaucratic responsibilities to these non-governmental organizations. The association system was founded in response to a 1907-08 diplomatic "Gentleman's Agreement" between Japan and the United States. The U. S. government insisted that all Japanese immigrants living in the United States be registered as aliens to provide a control for slowing down immigration. The agreement created an administrative challenge for the Japanese government because *Issei* were scattered throughout the western United States. To solve the problem of contacting all these thousands of *Issei*, a decision was made to delegate limited bureaucratic responsibilities to private associations made up of community leaders. These associations contacted their countrymen and processed their certificates of registration before passing them on to the Japanese consulate for approval. Both the central associations and their affiliated local associations shared the fees collected for this service thus providing financial stability for the organizations. It was a system of delegated authority and an important basis for the relationship between the Japanese government and the associations.[9]

The associations aided their communities in problems concerning the laws and customs in America as well as promoting friendly relations between the United States and Japan. Assistance was provided with certification of births and deaths, marriages and divorces, adoptions and inheritances.[10] The associations arranged for job opportunities. They did important work in lobbying against the exclusion movement that they eventually lost with the enactment of the Immigration Act of 1924.[11] The associations provided services to make life easier for the well-being of their immigrant community.

The Japanese Association of Oregon ceased operation as an organization in 1942. In 1951 the Portland Nikkei-Jin-Kai [Portland Japanese Ancestral Society] was organized and continues to serve the Japanese American community.[12]

1925: Japanese in Oregon Sawmills

W. G. Ide of the State Chamber of Commerce conducted a random survey in 1925 of Japanese employment in Oregon sawmills. There were approximately four thousand resident Japanese living in Oregon, many of whom had lived in Oregon for over twenty years and whose children were American citizens. In this survey, mill managers indicated that they preferred Japanese labor for green-chain work because of poor performance at that task by Caucasian labor and because the Japanese were culturally well-adapted to tasks requiring a high degree of cooperation and mutual support. These qualities made the *Issei* efficient workers on the green-chain and in demand in many Oregon mills (Table 4).

Table 4. Japanese Mill Employees
1925 Oregon Sawmills: A random survey

1. Clark and Wilson Lumber Company, Linnton, Oregon	50 Japanese
2. West Coast Lumber Company, Linnton,Oregon	50 Japanese
3. Crossett Lumber Company, Wauna, Oregon	50 Japanese
4. Westport Lumber Company, Westport, Oregon	40 Japanese
5. American Oregon Lumber Company, Vernonia, Oregon	20 Japanese
6. Long-Bell Lumber Company Longview, Washington	50 Japanese
7. Willamette Valley Lumber Company, Dallas, Oregon	10 Japanese
8. Peninsula Lumber Company Portland, Oregon	50 Japanese[13]
9. Oregon Lumber Company, Dee, Oregon	20 Japanese[14]

1926-1952: Civil Rights For Japanese Resident Aliens

Comments of Attorney Tim Willis
Corvallis, Oregon

The jury verdict in the Ogura case was never appealed, so no appellate court ever made a written analysis of the interesting legal issues arising out of the 1925 incident in Toledo, Oregon.

By pursuing the legal process to a jury verdict, Mr. Ogura, who was a Japanese citizen and a resident alien of Oregon, established his standing to sue in a U. S. court and to enforce his civil rights. Even though both the Oregon and U.S. Constitutions seemed to protect the rights of all resident aliens, Japanese resident aliens were treated differently than white resident aliens.

The post-Civil War amendments to the U.S. Constitution not only guaranteed the right of black citizens, but also of resident aliens, to due process of law. Amendment XIV of the U.S. Constitution included the following language: "[N]or shall any State deprive any person of life, liberty, or property, without due process of law; nor deny to any person within its jurisdiction the equal protection of the laws." (underlining added). Article I, Section 10 of the Oregon Constitution included similar language stating, "[E]very man shall have remedy by due course of law for injury done him in his person, property, or reputation." Thus the State and Federal Constitutions supported the rights of these Japanese resident aliens in Oregon to go to court for redress of the infringements on their persons, property rights, and rights to be employed. These constitutional provisions were not cited in the court pleadings or other documents filed in these five cases.

There may have been good reasons why constitutional law was not used. Since the inception of Oregon as a state in 1859, the Oregon Constitution had a definite racial bias favoring white aliens. Article I, Section 31, of the Oregon Constitution (now repealed) specifically dealt with the rights of aliens. The provision stated: "White foreigners who are or may hereafter become resident of this state shall enjoy the same rights in respect to repossession, enjoyment, and descent of property as native born-citizens." (underlining added). Given such racially biased language, the attorneys for these five Japanese litigants may well have decided to rely on treaty obligations instead of constitutional protections.

The court pleadings of the Japanese plaintiffs cited specific language from a 1911 treaty between the Imperial Government of Japan and the United States of America. The Treaty contained reciprocal language stating that the citizens of one country could receive in the other country "the most constant protection and security of their person and property, and shall enjoy in this respect the same rights and privileges as are or may be granted to native subjects or citizens." Earlier case law held that U. S. treaty rights had precedent over a state statute or constitution. The U.S.-Japanese treaty protected the civil rights of these Japanese resident aliens and was the basis used by these individuals to proceed in the court cases, which led to a jury verdict in one case and settlement in the other cases.

This small victory helped start a long process to establish equal treatment for resident aliens, no matter the race, color or creed. A number of subsequent legal obstacles had to be overcome. The 1924 Exclusion Act passed by Congress ended Japanese immigration to the U.S. until after World War II. Alien Land Laws were passed to prevent Japanese aliens from owning real property in Oregon. In 1939, the 1911 treaty between the Imperial Government of Japan and the United States (cited in the Ogura case pleadings) was terminated. The Nationality Act of 1940 prevented Japanese resident aliens from becoming naturalized citizens. They were now referred to as "ineligible aliens." In 1945 the Oregon Legislature passed an ancillary measure to the Alien Land Law which made it illegal to lease property to ineligible aliens or to their children, who were U. S. citizens, if the ineligible aliens would benefit. The 1949 Oregon Supreme Court decision in *Namba, et al v. McCourt and Neuner,* 185 Or 579, 204 P2d 569 specifically dealt with this issue. Etsuo Namba was born in Japan and was lawfully admitted to the United States. His son, Kenji Namba, was born in Multnomah County, Oregon, and was thus a U. S. citizen. Kenji Namba served as a member of the United States Army during World War II, engaged in combat operations in Italy, was honorably discharged from the Army, and returned to Multnomah County, Oregon to join his father in agricultural pursuits. The Oregon law had the effect of denying both of the Nambas the ability to lease property for farming purposes because Etsuo Namba, an ineligible alien, would benefit from the agricultural leases.

The Oregon Supreme Court overturned these Oregon laws. Chief Justice Rossman concluded his written opinion as follows:

> The several hundred alien Japanese to whom the Alien Land Law is applicable came to our state lawfully under law enacted by Congress. They are here lawfully and are entitled to remain. Many of them are parents of United States citizens, and some of them are mothers and fathers of American soldiers who gave a good account of themselves in the recent war.
>
> Our country cannot afford to create, by legislation or judicial construction, a ghetto for our ineligible aliens. And yet if we deny to the alien who is lawfully here the normal means whereby he earns his livelihood, we thereby assign to him a lower standard of bidding.
>
> We know of no basis upon which these two acts can be sustained.
>
> It is clear that [these Oregon laws infringe] upon the equal protection clause of the Fourteenth Amendment...
>
> We think that the analysis set forth in the preceding paragraphs show that our Alien Land Law...must be deemed violative of the principles of law which protect from classifications based upon color, race and creed.

In 1949 this Oregon appellate decision finally placed Japanese aliens on the same footing as any other alien, without further reference to color or creed.

NOTES

[1]Linda Tamura, "Railroads, Stumps and Sawmills: Japanese Settlers of the Hood River Valley," *Oregon Historical Quarterly* (Winter 1993-1994): 371.

[2]Eiichiro Azuma, "A History of Oregon's *Issei*, 1800-1952," *Oregon Historical Quarterly* (Winter 1993-1994): 318.

[3]Hosokawa, Bill, *Nisei: The Quiet Americans* (New York: Morrow, 1969), 56.

[4]*The Japanese American Community (a three generation study)*, Gene N. Levine Praeger Special Studies (New York: Praeger Publishers, 1981), 5.

[5]Kessler, Lauren, *Stubborn Twig* (New York: Penguin Books, 1993), 42.

[6]Eiichiro Azuma, "A History of Oregon's *Issei*, 1800-1952," *Oregon Historical Quarterly* (Winter 1993-1994): 358.

[7]Ichioka, Yuji, "Japanese Associations and the Japanese Government: A special relationship, 1909-1926," *Pacific Historical Review* (August, 1977):409.

[8]Ichioka, 410.

[9]Ichioka, 415.

[10]Ichioka, 418.

[11]Ichioka, 435.

[12]Doug Katagiri, "Nihonmachi," (Oregon Nikkei Legacy Center, Portland, Oregon, 2002), 5. Azuma, Eiichiro, "A History of Oregon's Issei, 1880-1952," *Oregon Historical Quarterly*, (Winter 1993-94): 366.

[13]"Survey Oriental Employment Mart," *Corvallis Gazette-Times*. Corvallis, Oregon. July 16, 1925.

[14]Homer Yasui, interview by author, written notes, Portland, Oregon, 15 April 2004.

Appendix B

(Charles) Daiichi Takeoka (1882-1954)

Photograph courtesy of the University of Oregon Knight Library

39. 1913–Oregana yearbook graduation picture, University of Oregon.

Daiichi Takeoka was born in 1882 in Hiroshima Prefecture, Japan. He left his family and immigrated to the United States in 1900 when he was eighteen years old.

After his arrival in the states, Takeoka not only adapted to the demands of a new culture, but also excelled in English. In a recent interview Kay Takeoka, Daiichi's son, spoke of the attention his father gave to his adopted language:

> Dad brought home from college a silver loving cup with his name inscribed on it. It was won in an oratorical competition.
>
> I can remember when he spoke at community functions. He would speak in English just as if he were born and raised over here. His command of English was very good.[1]

Takeoka's command of the English language aided him in his education.

Daiichi Takeoka graduated from the University of Oregon School of Law in 1912 (Photograph 39). Tim Willis, an attorney in Corvallis, Oregon, praised Takeoka's accomplishment:

> It was so impressive that a Japanese person graduated from law school in the early 1900s. There was nothing to help him succeed other than his own drive. The Japanese language and the English language are immensely different. For him to learn to speak English like a native-born American, he would have had to work incredibly

> hard. At that time there were not the aids that people have today. No television to listen to, no videotapes, no language courses.
>
> The other thing you have to realize is the difficulty of law school. Mr. Daiichi Takeoka not only had to learn another language but also had to learn the terminology and the thought process of a legal education. There is a lot of Latin thrown in and the courses are such that you are questioned, drilled and have to respond quickly in English. For him to be able to compete and succeed in law school was another level of challenge. He was absolutely a remarkable man.[2]

Takeoka's efforts to complete law school are even more remarkable since only American citizens could practice law in Oregon in the early 1920s. Takeoka completed a law degree his adopted state government wouldn't allow him to use.

Unable to practice law, but needing to provide for his family, Daiichi Takeoka turned to the farming business to earn his livelihood. Kay Takeoka discussed the work his father did:

> To support our family he became a broker for Swift and Company and sold fertilizer. He sold sacks of this and sacks of that to the farmers who raised strawberries and raspberries and to all the truck garden farmers in the Portland area.[3]

Through Daiichi's efforts the Takeoka family was able to live comfortably from his work as a broker. His job also allowed him time to serve his community.

Takeoka used his training to help his countrymen with various personal and community issues. In a recent interview Kay Takeoka mentioned one example:

> He was an important man for the *Issei* community. As kids I don't think that we really appreciated all that he had done. But I can see evidence of it in his activities with the community. For instance, when somebody would pass away and whether he knew them well or not, he always

> made it a point of going over and helping them out in their ceremonies for funerals and that sort of thing.[4]

Takeoka's commitment went beyond his studies to anyone in his community who might need help.

Since Takeoka could not join the Oregon Bar Association[5] he practiced unofficial law[6] out of his Portland office[7] with the help of a Caucasian named John H. Velie who acted in his behalf.[8] John Velie was the financial and employment representative for the Oregon Japanese Association at the time of the Toledo Incident.

During the Toledo Incident lawsuit in 1926, Takeoka signed affidavits on behalf of four of the plaintiffs to verify that they were Oregon residents. The plaintiffs no doubt appreciated Takeoka's efforts since they weren't able to leave their new jobs and travel to Portland to file the statement themselves.[9]

Takeoka remained active in legal issues involving his community and served as president of this association for a number of years. In 1923, he was involved in the unsuccessful attempt to prevent passage of the Oregon State Alien Land Law. The law had been written to make life difficult for *Issei* farmers wanting to buy or expand their farming operations. When a second and more restrictive Oregon State Alien Land Law was passed in 1945, Takeoka chaired a committee dedicated to overturning the unconstitutional law. By 1949 they had successfully challenged and nullified both the 1923 and the 1945 laws.[10]

Newspaper courtesy of
Homer and Miki Yasui family collection

Established 1904
THE OREGON NEWS
Published Daily, Except Sun
133 N. W. 2nd Ave. Portland, Ore.
M. Oyama, Owner and Publisher
Entered at Post Office at Portland, Oregon, as Second Class Mail Matter.

40. Taken from newspaper dated April 25, 1938

In 1952, after years of legal discrimination, the federal law that prohibited citizenship to *Issei* was repealed.[11] After decades of denial, Daiichi Takeoka became a United States citizen. He died only two years later on December 9, 1954 in Portland, Oregon.

Iwao Oyama (1889-1952) and *The Oshu Nippo*

For almost fifty years, a ten to twelve block area in downtown Portland, Oregon (mostly north of Burnside between Second and Sixth Avenues), was the heart of Portland's Japanese American community[12] known as Japantown (*Nihonmachi*). The area was home to *The Oshu Nippo* (*The Oregon News*). In 1917, Iwao Oyama became editor and publisher of *The Oregon News* and remained so until its closure in 1941.[13]

For almost four decades *The Oshu Nippo* (Photograph 40) was the only daily *Issei* newspaper published in Oregon. There were about fifteen employees, mostly women who hand-picked Japanese type from trays of individual lead characters. In addition to local news, Oyama reported the latest news from Japan, which he received daily through a radio news service based in Tokyo. The *Oshu Nippo* consisted of six pages, and was delivered daily to Japanese businesses in the

Photograph by Ted W. Cox—2004

41. June Schumann in front of the Merchant Hotel Building, October 28, 2004. She is holding a copy of the Oregon News dated April 15, 1938.

area and mailed throughout Oregon.[14]

In Photograph 41, June Schumann, Executive Director of the Oregon *Nikkei* Legacy Center is standing next to the original entrance of *The Oregon News* office, which was located in the now historic Merchant Hotel Building. She holds in her hands one of two known surviving issues of *The Oshu Nippo.*[15]

On December 7, 1941, the Federal Bureau of Investigation arrested Mr. Oyama for being a significant community leader and publisher of *The Oregon News*. All of his printing equipment was confiscated and never returned.

In 1945 following his wartime incarceration and detention, Mr. Oyama returned to Portland and established *The Oregon Nippo*, a semiweekly mimeographed newspaper that he published from a mezzanine office located in the grocery store at the Merchant Hotel.

On May 30, 1948, while living in the City of Vanport, (today the Delta Park area north of Portland) Oyama tragically lost his wife and home to a horrific flood that destroyed the whole town.[16] Many of his records were also lost in the flood.

On February 1, 1952 Mr. Oyama died of a heart attack. In 1983 the Oregon Lung Association nominated Iwao Oyama as a Notable Pioneer in Community Service.[17]

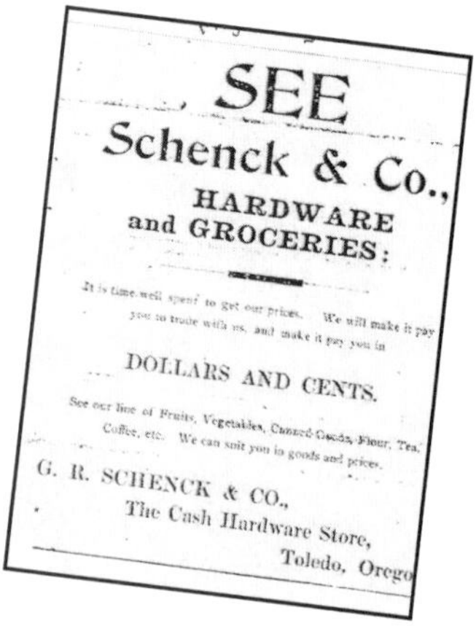

42. An advertisement in the August 31, 1900, Lincoln County Leader.

George R. Schenck (1867-1945)

Born October 19, 1867, in Iowa, George Schenck married Rosemary Coman in December 1899. After selling their Iowa farm, Schenck joined Rosemary in Toledo, where she had gone to get started in their new community. Together they had a son, George (Jack) Jackson.

Over the years, George Schenck was active in Toledo business. From 1900-1904 he owned a hardware and grocery store (Photograph 42). For four years he was a co-proprietor of a butcher shop. Schenck also worked as a carpenter, engineer and as an employee of the Toledo Electric Light Company. Between 1915-1933 he worked for the Toledo Police Department. On retirement from the police force, Schenck spent eight years working for C.D. Johnson Lumber as a timber guide.

George Schenck was also active in public service, serving on the Toledo City Council for two terms and as Fire Chief, Mayor, and Water Commissioner.[18]

Rosemary Coman Schenck (1879-1948)

Rosemary Coman was born May 20, 1879 in Monroe, Iowa. Her father was a member of the Iowa state legislature and had a significant influence on her interest in politics from an early age. As a young woman she studied journalism at Iowa State University, later writing for various newspapers including: the *Omaha Bee*, the *Call-Bulletin* (San Francisco) and the *Oregon Daily Journal*.

Rosemary Coman married George Schenck in 1899 in Iowa. She then moved to Toledo, Oregon, to get settled before George arrived. Their only child, Jack, served in World War II.

From 1902-1904 Rosemary Schenck worked with her husband in their store, Schencks & Co., on Hill Street where she added a millinery department. She also taught school in Siletz for a while.

As a part of her community service, Mrs. Schenck served

as State President of the Women's Relief Corps in the early part of the twentieth-century.

After being extremely active during the earlier Roosevelt campaign, in 1932 Rosemary Schenck became the Democratic candidate for State Senator. Her campaign energy did not pay off, however, as she lost the election. Four years later she was appointed Toledo Postmaster, which she remained until her accidental death in December 1948.[19]

Owen Hart (1902 - 1986)

Milton Owen Hart was born in Corvallis, Oregon on July 4, 1902. His family moved to Toledo in 1912. As a teenager, he decided to become a barber and started cutting hair when he was sixteen years old. In time he opened his own barbershop. Hart's Barbershop served Toledo for forty-nine years. In a 2004 interview, Sid Neal made the following comment about Owen:

> He was just a dandy person. . . a really nice person and a good barber. He would go and give haircuts at the hospital and even give free haircuts if somebody couldn't afford one.[20]

In addition to being a Toledo barber for almost half a century, Owen played a major roll in the development of the Toledo Fire Department.

When Owen was a teenager he often assisted firefighters with pulling the fire carts. In 1928 he formally joined the Toledo Volunteer Fire Department. He was the Toledo Fire Chief from 1936 to 1973.[21]

Hart served on the Toledo City Council from 1959 to 1965 and was a member of both the Toledo Fraternal Order of Eagles and Toledo Elks Lodge.

Owen Hart married Doris Smith in 1928, and they raised

three children: Larry, Rolland (Pug) and Jerolea.

Milton Owen Hart died on March 16, 1986 at his home in Toledo.[22]

NOTES

[1]Kay Takeoka, telephone interview by author, Alameda, California, April 19, 2004.

[2]Tim Willis, interview by author, written notes, Old World Deli, July 2004.

[3]Kay Takeoka, telephone interview.

[4]Kay Takeoka, telephone interview.

[5]Ito, Kazuo. *Issei: A History of Japanese Immigrants in North America*, (Japan Publication, Inc.) 1973, 161.

[6]Homer Yasui, interview by author, written notes, Portland, Oregon, April 8, 2004.

[7]Ito, 161.

[8]Kay Takeoka, telephone interview.

[9]Case #9710, National Archives-Pacific AK Region, Seattle, Washington. "Japanese win the first skirmish in big damage suit," *Lincoln County Leader,* 10 Dec 1925.

[10]Azuma, Eiichiro, "A History of Oregon's *Issei* 1880-1952," *Oregon Historical Quarterly* (Winter 1993-94): 356.

[11]Azuma, 358.

[12]Katagiri, Doug, *Nihonmachi: Portland's Japantown Remembered*, (Oregon *Nikkei* Legacy Center, 2002).

[13]Oyama, Albert, personal family records, July 2004.

[14]Oyama, family records.

[15]*The Oregon News,* 25 April 1938. Loaned for research courtesy of Homer and Miki Yasui.

[16]Abbott, Carl, *Portland Gateway to the Northwest* (California: American Historical Press, 1997), 121.

[17]Oyama, family records.

[18]"George R. Schenck, County Pioneer, Succumbs Tuesday," *Lincoln County Leader*, 2 August 1945.

[19]"Postmaster's Rites Held," *Newport News*, 23 December 1948.

[20]Neal, Sid, interview by author, tape recording, Toledo, Oregon, May 20, 2004.

[21]"Toledo Fireman Recalls Early Department Days," *Newport News-Times*, October 1975.

[22]"Milton Owen Hart," *Newport News-Times*, March 1986.

Appendix C

Copies of Original Japanese Newspaper Articles

The following article was translated and is included here for reference and interest, but was not used in the body of the book (Translation #13).

Translation #13

Translation by Hiroko Takada Amick and Glen-Paul Amick.

The Great Northern Daily News
(Taihoku Nippo)
July 24, 1926

Toledo Incident Trial
Japanese win trial
Yesterday afternoon the trial results were presented.

The six Toledo defendants will have to pay the plaintiff, Mr. T. Ogura $2,500.
Another trial is scheduled to begin around November.
From the Portland Branch

Summary of the Trial:

First: Mr. Ogura sued for $25,000 and he won $2,500.

Second: The deliberation was 2 hours 31 minutes.

Third: the Japanese have the right to work anywhere, anytime and at any pay rate. The plaintiff lawyer is satisfied with the winning results.

Fourth: the defendant's lawyer has until September 1st to appeal.

Fifth: It is hoped that this trial will make good will between Japan and United States and for all the different races living in the country for race relations.

Since the 12th of July when the trial started it took nine trial days to finish the trial in Portland under Federal Court Judge Wolverton. The trial finished Friday July 23rd. Attorney Collier for the Japanese spoke for about an hour in summary.

At 1:30 in the afternoon Judge Wolverton talked to the twelve members of the jury. He started to read the legal rights of the Japanese-Americans from the Japanese treaty between the two countries. It was stated that when a mob tries to pursue its selfish goals it is wrong. The mob hurt the plaintiffs both physically and mentally.

Judge Wolverton suspended the trial at 2 pm for deliberation. Around 5 pm a decision was announced that Mr. Ogura won the trial and that the defendant had to pay $2,500. The Defendants were W. S. Colvin, George Schenck, Rosemary Schenck, Owen Hart, Frank Sturdevant, H.T. Pritchard.

There are four more Japanese who have suits:

Ichiro Kawamoto is suing for $25,000

Ito Kawamoto is suing for $30,000

Youjiro Mitani is suing for $25,000

Masumi Tsuboi [Matsuto Tsubokawa] is suing for $25,000

July 24, 1926, Page 2

Their trial starts in November after the court's summer break.

Summary of what occurred.

Plaintiff Tamakichi Ogura and the other Japanese were hired to work for the Spruce Mill in Toledo, Oregon on the date of July 13, 1925.

The mill built houses for them. Two wives of the workers were hired to cook for the workers. Mrs. (Kawamoto) and three children were there when the incident happened.

The Toledo people had a meeting to discuss the company's plan to hire Japanese. These people gathered signatures for a petition against the Japanese coming. They had various meetings. There was a meeting on July 11th 1925 at the city baseball park and the following day a meeting held at the waterfront.

A couple of hundred people went to the mill, where deputies tried to stop them. The deputies told the mob that they could not meet with the Japanese and a fight ensued. The mob then went to the Japanese compound and took the Japanese belongings and put them into a truck and shipped them to Corvallis. The Japanese were placed into cars and also sent to Corvallis.

Some of the mob gave money to the Japanese.

The governor of the state and the senator for the county and the Japanese consul had previously been asked by the Toledo people not to allow the Japanese workers to come. They have been accused of threatening the Japanese.

This incident might be a problem between the United States and Japan. The two governments discussed this problem. The Japanese government also discussed this issue with the Oregon State Governor.

This was an international issue and the two governments were meeting to try and resolve it.

The plaintiffs' lawyer, Collier said that the case was not about how much the Japanese were awarded but the fact that if the Toledo people had won this trial, then other people would think that they would have the right to prohibit Japanese from working anywhere in the United States. This would be against the legal rights of the Japanese people under the provisions of the Japanese American Treaty. So the Japanese won the rights for the Japanese and Japanese-Americans to live and work in the U.S. freely. Attorney Collier was satisfied with the results.

Copies of *The Great Northern Daily News* can be found on microfilm at the University of Washington Libraries, Special Collections, Seattle.

Original #1

July 13, 1925 — Page 1

The Great Northern Daily News.

Monday JULy 13 1925

同胞働人二十餘名郡外に放逐さる

暴徒四百名製材所へ押寄せ
會社番人等を擲ぐり倒す

數週前以來の葛藤

オレゴン州トレドのパシフイツク、スプルース會社と一部勞働者との間に數週以前より製材所に日本人を使用する件につきて意見を異にしたるが其の結果は遂に去る土曜に至り拳鬪流血の慘を見るに至り爭鬪の末

暴徒は日本人を狩り集めて其の所持品と共に自動車とトラックとに積みリンコルンの郡外へ送り出したる珍事ありたり

會社へ押寄せる以前にストリートに於て村民大會開かれ此會には煽動者の熱狂的演說あり集會せるは婦人小兒をも併せて四百人許りなりしが先頭に立てる一人米國々旗を翻へし人々之に從ひ日本人の居る方面へ進

打したり

會社に雇はれたる番人等は武器を携へ居り暴徒の進み來るや其の首領株に面會し會社の敷地內に入り來るべからずと警告したるも大浪の押せたるが如く暴徒は其の言を耳にもかけず血に武器をも奪取りて之を構內に投げ棄て會社側の人々と暴徒と入り亂れ打ちつ打たれつ双方共に血を流せるもの數名に及びたるが闘は只拳のみにて行はれ武器を使用したるものなし

會社々長シー、デー、デーンツンを始めとして會社の人々は暴徒に道理を說き聞かさんとせるも暴徒の喊聲に音聲聞かず其の內に暴徒の首領株は日本人の居る方へ入り日本人へ所持品を取纏め待ち合せる自動車及びトラックにて郡外へ立退くべしと告げ日本人は敢て抵抗せんとせず從順に立退きたり

セリフのホースフォール氏は部下のものと現場へ驅け付けマーチン、ガーマーとチヤーレス、エー、バツタとダブルユー、エス、コルヴアー、の三人を拘引し群集に退散を命じ群集は不承無承に退散せり

煽動者の姓名五十名以上はセリフに書き取られたれば彼等は其れ〳〵所罰せらるゝならん其內投獄されたるもあり

パシフイツク、スプルース會社は數週以前に同製材所のグリーン、チエーン、ヂヤンダスとして知られたる部分の仕事に日本人を雇ひ入るゝ計畫なる旨を聲明せり此部の仕事は普通の賃金にては白人勞働者を雇入るゝこと能はざりしなり

此聲明には大反對あり去

English translation found on page 66.

Original #1

July 13, 1925 — Page 2

る木曜日に約十五名の日本人をぽーとランドより入れ來り形勢切迫したり會社側は官憲や郡內ビヂネスマンと問題を討議したるに說は一致を見ざりしなり記者曰く（右はオレゴニアンに載せる特信なるが去六月二十九日の本紙第八面に掲載せるぽートランド通信には二十六日の夜トレド商業會議所及び同所實業協會は日本人雇入問題につき集會を催し熟議の結果双方了解を得て日本人を雇入るゝことゝなりたる旨、報じたり）

會社に使用 する人數は一千名以上リンコルン郡內第一の納稅者なり社長ヂョンソンは曰く此珍事ありしは甚だ悲しむべきことなるも會社に非難の點なしと思ふ何となれば會社は日本人を使用せねば仕事が出來ないから使用したるなり云々

聯合通信社 トレド十二日發信によれば暴徒の數は二百五十名なりしと

本社支社より

本朝電話にて

右の事件につき本朝十一時ぽーとランド支社よりの電話によれば放逐されたる人數は日本人二十二名、コレアン一名、ヒリッピン四名合計二十七名なるが彼等は自動車にて其の荷物はトラックにてトレドより五十哩のコーヴアリスまで送られ同所より鐵道にてぽーとランドへ歸着し只今長谷川商店に集合して善後策研究中なるが損害は會社側へ請求する筈又オレゴン州商業會議所書記長アイゾー氏は本事件に關して本朝セーラムに於て知事ピヤス氏及び上院議員マクナリー氏と會見し協議する筈なりと

騷動の原因 は人種問題にあらずトレド地方に白人の求職者多く此上の勞働者を採入せずとも充分にありといふにありと

English translation found on page 66.

Original #2

July 15, 1925 — Page 1

同胞放逐事件

大北日報

日本人二十二名外に朝鮮人一名、比島人四名（昨紙掲載東京發信に三十五名とあるは誤）オレゴン州トレドより、暴徒の爲に放逐せられたる事件は、未だ如何に解決せらるゝやを耳にせざるも、セーラム十四日發電に州勞務官グラム氏より、會社と白人勞働者との葛藤事件は恐く平和の解決を見るべしと、知事ピーヤス氏へ語りたりといふ

平和解決とは如何。未だ具體的に之を明白にすること能はざるも日本人側の關する限りにては、暴徒少くとも其巨魁は相當の所罰を受け、放逐されたる日本人に對しては其損害を賠償さるべく、且つ今後斯る事件の、再び發生せざるやう、相當の注意を加へらるゝ乎、若くは斯る場合に官憲より相當の保護あるべき保證ある乎は、蓋し至當の解決なるべしと思はる

若し然らずして、暴徒にして不問に置かれ日本人の損害に對して賠償されず、又將來の保障も無からんには、日本人の權利は全く沒却されたりと謂ふべし

今回の事件を以て、人種的排所にあらずして、日本人は白人勞働者と會社との葛藤に捲き添へを喰ひしといふの嫌もあり、會社の聲言する所によれば、同社が東洋人を雇入れたるは、白人勞働者の好まざる仕事即ちリーン、チェーンに働かせる爲にして、東洋人を雇はざれば働く者なく、會社は經營難に陷るべしといふにあり、又暴徒の擧言する所によれば、白人勞働者は有り餘る程あり、會社は將來白人勞働者の賃金を下げんとする手段に東洋人を雇入れたるなりと

會社と白人勞働者との言ひ分は何れが事實なるやを知らざるも、斯る場合に他地方より勞働者の入込める時は、其日本人なると白人なるとを問はず一切之を排斥すること。先年の鐵道ストライキに、華州ノーバーンに

於て東洋貿易會社の入れ込めるストライキ、ブリーカーを排斥したるが如き性質のものならんには之を人種戰にあらずして、經濟戰なりと稱すべく、若し又先年加州ターロックに起りたる日本人放逐事件の如く、其仕事口を白人勞働者に奪ひ取らんとして、行はれたらんには、之を人種戰と稱すべし

今回放逐されたる日本人は、ストライキ、ブリーカーとして雇はれしにあらざるが如し、況んや理不盡にも脅迫的に放逐するに至りては、之を輕々に看過すべきにあらず、

放逐が平和手段にて行はれ、暴力に訴ふることなかりしは、不幸中の幸といふべく、況んや暴徒も日本人が從順に立退くことを快諾したるにもの丶哀れを感じ、旅費の一端を醵出して之を差出せると、日本人が之を其儘慈善團體へ寄附せよとて手にせざりしは、（手にせざりしも慈善團体へ寄附せよと言ひ

English translation found on page 69.

Original #2

July 15, 1925 — Page 2

しは一旦受取りしに當る事ろ受
取らず」と斷言しゐる方宜しかり
しと思はる）彼の太田の殿に於
ける、責任觀念の和歌の詠み交
はし、又源平須磨の戰に於ける
熊谷敦盛の情けに似たる趣あ
り、一佳話たるを失はざるも、
此時若し日本人が會社の門番等
の如く、暴徒の言に從はず、立
退くことを肯んぜざりしならば
暴徒は暴力的に放逐し暴行をも
加へたらんと想像するに難から
ず。暴動煽動者等が、其始めに過言
を以て立退きを請求せるは、是
亦一種の脅迫に外ならず。中間
の一佳話ありしも、事件全般が
脅迫的放逐なりしことを看過す
べからず

吾々在留日本人は、太平洋沿
岸其他の地方にありて、既に法
律によりて農業に從事すること
を拒まれたり。今又脅迫的に工
業勞働に從事することを拒まる
斯くして其生活の範圍を縮小せ
られ行く時は、其前途案じて如
何ん

東京政界筋によれば、日本外務
省は、此度の事件を重大視せず
冷靜の態度を持すといふ。無能
なる官吏が、冷靜の名に隱くれ
無責任を以て事に臨み、其職
分を怠りて恥づることを知らざ
るは古今同慨、斯る外務省を有
する吾人海外在留者は自から心
細さを感ぜざるを得ず

由來外國人として、種々の不
便を忍び、不利を蒙り居る吾人
は、其本國政府により條約上
の權利を保護せらるゝにあらず
んば、立つ瀬のなき身なり

多人數のあり。正當に生活の
途を講ぜんとして、暴徒に脅迫
的放逐を喰ひし時、其本國政府
が重大事件にあらずとして、外
國官憲の爲すがまゝに任せんと
する態度を執ることあらば、吾
人は政府の保護の下にあるや否
やを疑はざるを得ず

English translation found on page 69.

Original #3

July 13, 1926

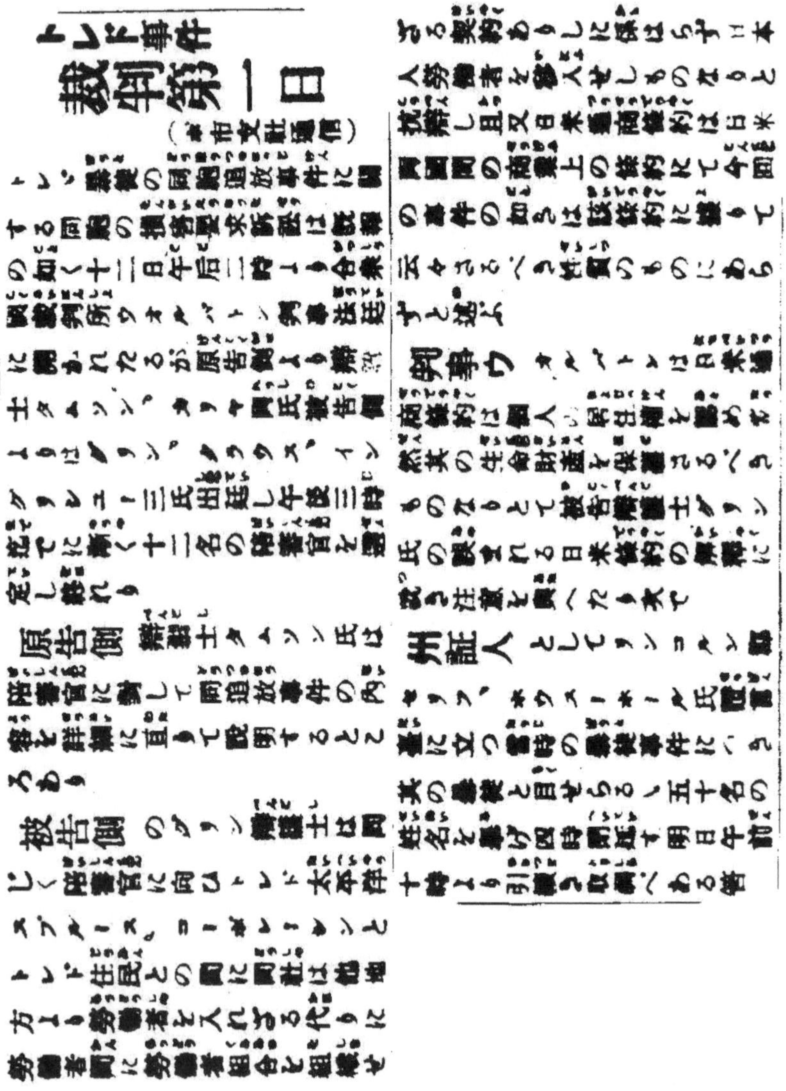

トレド事件
裁判第一日
（桑市支社通信）

トレド暴徒の同胞追放事件に関する同胞の損害賠償要求訴訟は既報の如く十二日午後二時より合衆国裁判所ウォルバートン判事法廷に開かれたるが原告側より弁護士タムソン、キリヤ両氏被告側よりはグリン、グラウス、インダリソユー三氏出廷し午後三時迄でに漸く十二名の陪審官を選定し終れり

原告側　弁護士タムソン氏は陪審官に対して同追放事件の内容を詳細に亘りて説明するところあり

被告側　のグリン弁護士は同じく陪審官に向ひトレド太本件はスプティース、コーボレーシヨンとトレド住民との間に同社は地方より労働者を入れざる代りに労働者間に労働者組合を組織せざる契約ありしに係はらず日本人労働者を雇入せしものなりと抗弁し且つ又日米通商条約は日米両国間の商業上の条約にて今回の事件の如きは該条約に拠りて云々さるべき性質のものにあらずと述ぶ

判事ウォルバートンは日米通商条約は個人の居住権を認め於其の生命財産を保護さるべきものなりとて被告弁護士グリン氏の誤まれる日米条約の解釈に就き注意を与へたり次で

州証人としてリンコルン郡キリフ、ホウスーホーメ氏証言台に立つ当時の暴徒事件にへつ其の暴徒と目せらるゝ五十名の姓名を挙げ四時閉廷す明日午前十時より引続き取調べある筈

English translation found on page 92.

Original #4
July 14, 1926

トレド事件
裁判第二日
（ポートランド支社通信）

午後二時 より引續き開廷され原告川本一郎氏は證言臺に立ちて昨年七月十二日は數十名の暴徒は星條旗を先導に立て列をなして日本人キャンプを襲ひ立退きを脅迫し無理矢理に自動車に乗せ同胞が所持の荷物は暴徒にて処理して同じゝ自動車に積んで郊外コーパリスまで追放されたる當時の模樣を詳細にわたりて申立て終り

トレドの パシフィック、スプルース會社の副社長兼總支配人なるジョンソン氏は證言臺に上り當日暴徒一團は國旗を先導に會社の所有地に侵入し來りたるが爲め侵入を防がんとなしたるも其れが爲め却つて同會社の雇人なるレチャルトン、マーカム、ホーレマンの三名は暴徒の爲め負傷を蒙りたりとて暴徒の巨魁とも見做すべき被告の件名を列擧して暴徒の一團中にありたりとて約一時間にわたりて原告に頗る有力なる證言を陳述了つて十分間休憩來て

同會社の レッピング、クラークのマクマール 氏は證言臺に立ち當時の模樣及び昨年七月十一日にトレドに於てマス、ミーチングを催せりと是又原告側に有力なる證言をなし被告側グリン辯護士は同胞自發的にトレドを立退きたるもの丶如く論爭せんとするに對し原告側辯護士ガリガー氏は當時のマス、ミイテングに使用せし貼紙を證據として提供し日本人放逐は暴行前に於て既に計畫されたるものなりと一矢を酬ひ四時四十分閉廷を宣し十四日午前十時より引續き開廷する筈當日

傍聽席は 立錐の地なき程多數の日白人であつた

English translation found on page 94.

Original #5

July 15, 1926 — Page 1

トレド事件

裁判第三日

（ポートランド支社通信）

午後二時より引續き開廷最初に證言臺に立ちたるはミセス、アルバーリーといふ美しき婦人なり此人の證言によれば暴徒が日本人を襲撃する以前に二人の米國人はヒドイ醜い言葉て會話をしてゐた其れから暫くして約三百名の暴徒が押寄せて來た被告の一人オーウエン、ハートは米國旗を振りかざして居た一人は何回もピストルを發射して居た云々次に

川本一郎氏 のミセスが證言臺に上り通辯を通じて其夫及び同女の暴行を受けたることを證言し中途にて感極まつて泣いた時には傍聽人一同互に何事がさゝやいて居た餘程皆んなに感動を與へた樣子てあつた同女の證言要領は

一人の日本 人は血を出して居たのを見た又七人の白人が無理に仝女の家へ押入り其夫を擲ぐり倒し血を流した夫は二人の米國人に家から引張り出され自分も子供と共に家外へ出て又洗濯ものヽラインにあつたのを取つて同女の顔へ投げつけた米國人男女三名があつた云々次にニウポート、ニウス社のマレウマレウス氏が證言した其要領

私は被告の 面體を知つて居るが日本人に害を加へたのは觀なかつた次に通信員レスターマーチン證言す其要領に曰くエツテ、デヤーマーが暴徒の首魁と思はれた又會社の人は鼻から血を出すのがあつた又日本人を自動車で逐ひ出すと云つて居たのもあつた

原告辯護士 が證人を出すのは午三后時半て一段落となつたので次に被告辯護士グリーンは起つて申請して曰く只今までの證言てはミセス、スケンクに對しては何等日本人に損害を與へて居ない依つて裁判長は直に仝女に對して判決を下されたい

裁判長は此 申請を拒絶したので次にグリーン辯護士から被告全部に對して直に判決を下されんことを申請したが是亦拒絶された依つて

被告側の證 人を出した其證人はハリー、ブリツチヤドといふ人で此人の證言は七月十一日の夜の集會には七十人はかり

English translation found on page 95.

Original #5

July 15, 1926 — Page 2

業主ら會社の雇入れた日本人に
地方の樣子を聞き其在留するこ
とは地方民の好まざることを申
聞かせ自から納得して退去して
貰ふことゝ又武器を携帶せぬこと

其れから翌日會社へ談判

に行る日本人通譯を出して貰ひ
度いといふと云つたのに會社長は
直ちに立ち去れ若し立ち去らざ
れば今前等六人位殺されても構
は沈黙にありと一同を怒らせた
といふ事などを語り其經過中簡
てタイムが來たので閉會 に な
つれ

今十五日は 全鐵材所で臨
化の試驗があるのでトレド事件
全判は休み

English translation found on page 95.

Original #6

July 16, 1926

トレド同胞放逐事件

熱火の如き公判（二）

妻と共に家から引摺り出された

太平洋スプルース、コーポレーション總支配人デーン、デロンソン氏は語を續けて曰く暴徒は日本人の家ともを取巻いて其れから日本人共を家の前へ狩り出した其時セリフのホーストフオールと副セリフのゼス、ダニエルスとが到着した其れからデャーマーとエルヴインとを拘引したダニエルは兩人を引張つて行きホーストフオールは其邊の人々の姓名を手帳に書き取つた群衆は四散し出したがデャマーとコルヴインとは後戻りして左の如く叫んだ

「來れ人々よチヤツプはまだ出で

行かなかつたが午後に出て行くんだ」この時シー、デーはホースフールに云つた「セリフよ予は此プロパチー（動産と不動産と）を君に渡す」云々其れから吾等は事務所の方へ去つた四十五分程ど經てから私共は暴徒が日本人を小隊のやうにしてトラツクを下の方へ引張つて行くのを見たプラットフオームに居た人々は喝采して其等も後からついて行つた一人の

日本婦人 は家の前に同女の行李を置きラインから洗濯物を取り入れつゝあつた其處を男女の白人が通つてラインから洗濯物を引たくり之を此日本婦人の顔に投げつけ「ソラお前は何か忘れて居た」と言つた

午前中に は原告小倉玉吉氏が證言したが午後には川本一郎氏の證言があつた川本氏は中々よく分かつて居る證人であつた同氏は六十人の勞働者を會社へ供給すべく契約して居る人であるが其證言に曰く小石や木片が雨の如くに日本人キャンプへ投げつけられ同氏は暴徒の爲につき倒され

家から引摺り出されて鼻から血

が出た同氏の妻君も引出されて愛飼して居た小犬は盗まれ或白人何名かは會社の構内に於ける鬪爭に負傷した川本氏曰く「自分は二分間の内に其家から出て行けと言はれたから何故かと尋ねたら理由は何てあつてもかもはない吾等は最早や日本人が此邊に居るのを許さない」と答へた私は言ふやう私は製材所に勤して居るから此處に止まる云々彼等曰く

『貴樣コゝを立去らないと首を吊

して殺して仕舞ふぞ」と言ひながら兩人して私をフロアへ打倒し私を引摺つて家から外へ出し又彼等は私の妻をも引摺り出した云々

English translation found on page 99.

Original #7
July 17, 1926 — Page 1

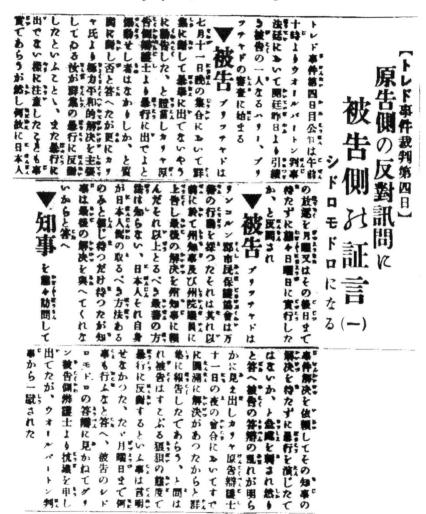

【トレド事件裁判第四日】

原告側の反對訊問に 被告側の証言

シドロモドロになる(一)

トレド事件第四日目公判は午前十時よりウォールバートン判事法廷において開廷昨日より引續き被告の一人なるハリー、ブリッチヤードの審査に始まる

▼被告 ブリッチヤードは七月十一日晩の集合において群集に對して暴擧に出でないやうに勸告した、と證言しカツヤ原告側辯護士より暴行に出でよと煽動せし者はなかりしか、と質問に對し否と答へたが更にカツヤ氏より極力平和的解決を主張してゐる汝が群集の暴行に反對したといふことゝ、また暴行に出でない様に注意したことも事實であらうが然し何故に日本人の放逐を月曜又はその後日まで待たずに昨今日曜日に實行したか、と反問され

▼被告 ブリッチヤードはリンコルン郡市民保護協會は万一群集の行動を懼つたそれは其れ以前に於て州知事及び州院議員に上告し最後の解決を州知事に頼んだそれ以上とるべき最善の方法は知らない、日本人それ自身が日本人側の取るべき方法あるのあと信じ待つだけ待つたが知事は最後の解決を與へてくれないからと答へ

▼知事 を昨今訪問して事件解決を依頼してその知事の解決を待たずに暴行を演じたてはないか、と金曜を興され然りと答へ被告の答辯の亂れが明らかに見え出しカツヤ原告辯護士十一日の夜の會合においてすでに圓滿に解決があつたからと群衆に報告したてあらう、と問はれ被告はすこぶる狼狽の態度で暴行に反對するといふ事は言明せなかつた、たゞ月曜日まで何事も行ふなと答へ、被告のレドロモドロの答辯に見かねてグリン被告側辯護士より抗議を申し出てたが、ウォールバートン判事から一蹴された

English translation found on page 101.

Original #7

July 17, 1926 — Page 2

▼原告 側辯護士カッチャ

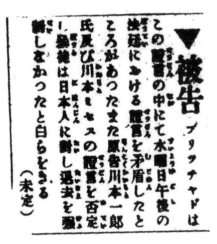

側は原告の證言を繰り返へして日本人の放逐狀況をのべ被告が月曜日まで行動を待つといふ意思を有し、かつまた暴行に反對しながら日曜日に暴徒が大擧して日本人キャンプを襲ふたてはないかとの問に日本人に會って説明したいがため行ったと質問に應じたがこれがため二百五十名の人間が必要か、と問れ群衆の數は正確に知らぬが一人で行くと日本人が事件を重大視せないから七十五名の人間が二十九名の日本人に說明に行つたのかと皮肉つれる

▼被告 ブリッチャドは

この證言の中にて水曜日午後の法廷における證言を矛盾したところがあつたまた原告川本一郎氏及び川本ミセスの證言を否定し暴徒は日本人に對し退去を強請しなかつたと白らをきる

（未定）

English translation found on page 101.

Original #8

July 19, 1926 — Page 1

The Great Northern Daily News.

Monday JULy 19 1926

大北日報

トレド事件

一個年前、オレゴン州トレドに於て、日本人及び朝鮮人男女数十名が、暴徒の為に、理不盡にも、郡外へ放逐せられたる事件は、當時日米兩國政府の注目を惹き、日本政府は、米國政府へ何等かの交渉を開き、米國政府は、央州知事へ向つて交渉するところありしとの報ありしも官憲の暴徒を拘引したる事を聞かず。又何等刑法上の手續を取りたるを聞かず、然るに被害日本人の内五名のものは、暴徒の巨魁と認むべきもの六名を相手取り、合衆國區裁判所に、損害賠償の訴訟を提起し、現に其公判が、ポートランドに於て開かれ居ること、本紙連日報道の通

りなり

裁判の性質上、原被両造の申立てに、大なる相違あり、一方は排斥されて、郡外に放逐せられたることを立證せんとし、一方は放逐せるにあらずして、東洋人の隨意に立退きたることを立證せんとしつゝあり、判決の如何は、證據次第なるべければ吾人は敢て其判決如何を推測せんと試むるものにあらず、只今日まで法廷に於て、證言せられたる内、双方の證言の一致せる點につきて、吾人の所見を述べんとす

一方の證人の述べたる事を、他の一方の證人が反對せず、双方に於て事實と認め居る事は恐く左の通りならん

太平洋スプールス、ローボレーションに、東洋人を雇入れたるは、トレド住民の好まざるところ、住民は何卒して、東洋人を雇はしめざるやうに、知事や領事に面會を求めて、其意見を述べ、又合衆國上院議員へも書面にて助力を求めたるに其効ありしを以て、郡民大會を開きて東洋人を去らしむる方法を講じ豫定の行動を執り、大勢の者共米國旗を先頭に押し立て、コーポレーション構内へ押寄せ、其或る者はジャップをやっつけろと呼びつゝ會社の構内にて會社のものと格闘して血を流し、次いで日本人住宅區へ殺倒し、時を移さずして、住民側の雇ひたる自動車に、荷物もろ共に東洋人全部を載せ、郡境界線の外に運するや、其處に下車せしめたり

English translation found on page 103.

Original #8

July 19, 1926 — Page 2

右は双方の証人の申立ての中
其一致點を抽出したるものなる
が、之に由りて吾人は、住民側
に於て東洋人の入り來るを嫌ひ
しことの、頗る強烈なりしを知
りたり
　東洋人としては、斯る不人氣
の所へ入り込むことは、假令資
本家の歡ぶことならんも、賢明
なる仕方にあらず、若し又入込
む前に、土地の人氣如何を知ら
ざりしならば、資本家又は何人
かに騙られたるなるべし。日本
領事は、特に勞働者側の陳述
を聞き居りしといへば、之も注
意が足らざりしことを、後に知
り得たるなるべし
　土地の人々にしても、大勢押
し寄せて。立退かしむる手段を
取りたることは、万策盡きたる
上のことゝ彼等は思ひしならん
も未だ執るべき策は盡きしには
あらざりしならん
　東洋人勞働者が、白人勞働者
と一所になりて、資本家に楯つ
く場合ありとも、資本家もよく
考ふれば、其れは自衞上無理な
らぬことゝ觀察するならんも。
之と反對に、東洋人勞働者が資
本家と一所になりて、白人勞働
者に敵對する時は、白人勞働者
の怒りは、甚だ强よかるべく時
には暴行に出でんも知るべか
らず
　華州に於ても、一昨年鐵道に
働ける日本人が、勞資双方の板
挾となりて、苦しき立場に置か
れたることあり、勞資間の爭
には勞働者は勞働者同志一所に
なることは、原則として正しき
ことゝなり

English translation found on page 103.

Original #9
July 20, 1926 — Page 1

The Great Northern Daily News.

Tuesday JULy 20 1926

ポートランド「十九日」

トレド事件
公判第五日

トレド事件の裁判は本日午後二時よりクオートン判事法廷に於いて引續き開廷されたが傍聴席は日白人で一杯であつた

▽被告側証人
として元太平洋

スプルース、コーポレーションに働らいて片腕を失なつたアジヤコーブソンが證言臺に上り自分は群集の集合に加はつたが群集は日本人に對して暴行を加へなかつたと原告側の申し立てを否定した原告側カリヤ辯護士はジヤコーブソンに向つて群集は日本人に對して何か話さなかつたかと質問したがジヤコーブソンは群集は何も云はなかつたが白人と日本人は會話をしてゐたそれは日本人がトレドを引き揚げたから太平洋スプルース、コーポレーションを辭たへるといつてゐたと答へた會話を変へてゐた白人と日本人はたれであつたかと原告側辯護士から反問されて三十フイト許り離れてゐたから判らなかつたと逃げ、長らくトレドに居住してゐて僅かに三十フイト位ゐの距離で離てあるが判らぬとは矛盾を突かれた揚句知らなかつたと向ふを切つて引下る

▽トレド週刊
新聞記者ジーメブ

パーキール吹いて證言したが自分は事件のあつた後の三時過ぎに現場に行つたのであるが日本人を排斥せよといふ言葉は聞かなかつたと被告側のために陳じ本事件には絶對に關係がないと主張しカリヤ原告側辯護士より大會に使用した[illegible]はり紙をつきつけられて誰に頼まれて印刷したものかと質問され自分記者であつて知らぬが兄弟が印刷したものだらうと曖昧に答へ

▽知事より某
所への報告に依

ると州知事秘書官デルゼル氏が事件勃發の後トレドに出張せる際に事件の煽動者と目せらるゝスケンク宅に會合を催して其の善後策に就いて協議せし際出席してゐたではないかと訊問され自分は新聞記者として出席したと白[illegible]たが原告側辯護士の訊問に[illegible]ドムトレド市民[illegible]會員だと自白した

English translation found on page 106.

Original #9

July 20, 1926 — Page 2

▽右證言終つて同胞を自動車

でコーパリスまで運んだといふ證人の一人であるオーユン、ハートの兄弟であるアルシー・ハート證言台に上り自分は事件の起つた夜そろは野球グランドに行つてゐて事件の模様は知らぬが事件のあつた後に日本人がタウンにゐたからコーパリスまで自動車で連れて言つたと證言原告辯護士からたれに頼まれて自動車で運んだかと反問されタウンの人が頼んだから連れて行つたと答へ暴徒からかと聞かれてノーと答へしかし自動車で運んだが金はもらはなかつたと證言

▽被告オーエン、ハートの

證言に移つたが被告は低能的な微笑を浮べすこぶる不眞面目な態度で自分は會社側の番人と喧嘩してブラツクアイを喰はされたが自分も會社の番人を擲つてやつたしかし後から會社側の番人は拳手を出さなかつたと證言し本事件にもつとも重大のボイ

English translation found on page 106.

Original #10

July 21, 1926 — Page 1

The Great Northern Daily News.

Wednesday JULy 21 1926

トレド事件
公判第六日
（○市支社通信）

火曜日の公判に第一に被告弁護士の指図によりて証人台に上りたるはタユンデンノの牧師レーデー、モリスで此人は昨年七月にはトレドの美以教会で牧教して居た又兼ねてトレド商業会議所の幹事をもやつて居た被告弁護士は「貴下の商業会議所勤務中に役員は日本人労働者に関する何等かの行動を執つたか」と質疑したが原告弁護士の反対で証人の答弁はなかつた

トレドから コーヴァリスまで二人の日本人を送つたビーアイ、マフキンタイルといふ男は誰にも頼まれず又運び賃も取らずに送つたと証言しトレド森林会社及家具屋の妻君ミセス、エセル、ベートマンといふは例のリンコルン郡市民保護団と幹事補の一人であつたが

被告スケンノ夫人の為に証言したと思はれたベートマン夫人は曰ふ日曜日（騒動のあつた日）の午後二時から四時までの間自分はミセス、スケンノの家に居た其時傍に男女数名も同席して知事や上院議員マクナリ[illegible]ーラムに訪問して日本人労働者のことを話すことについての計画を相談したと証言したが火曜日に被告側で重要の証人として出したのはトレドのコントラクターのアーサー、イー、マーヴインであつた氏は昨年七月十二日午后の騒動をヌッカー自ら目撃したといひ最初大勢が会社の前を突破したことから語り出し日本人区域へ押寄せたことを語り被告弁護士の質問に答へて更に乱棒めくことなく日本人は形勢を見て自から出て行つたやうに証言した其大要を左に記さんマーヴイン曰く「以上の争闘の後会社の当局者は何等の抵抗を試みず吾等は日本人区域へ乗込んだヂャップスは彼等の家の内に居た家の中から一人が出て来たり話しをした其人は大勢押しかけたは何故かと尋ねたので其れはトレドに彼等の居ることを好まないからだと言ひ聞かされた之に答へて彼の日本人は「吾々は去る」と云ひ其れから家々の戸をノックして此事を彼の国人に告げた」と証言し.

English translation found on page 109.

Original #10

July 21, 1926 — Page 2

末
れから藤吉藤富士との関係にま
つた
「日本人の家の戸又は窓のどれでも決して開けられたりしたれ乎
「ノー
「窓又は戸のどれでもお辞かれた乎
「ノー
「どの日本人でも荒々しく取扱はれたのを見た乎
「ノー
「政府は日本人は群衆の中に交つて居た乎
「イエス
「どの日本人でも其興国又は太陽に自の傷して居たのを見た乎
「ノー
「日本人は路上に於て追まされるか又は脅迫されたれ乎
「ノー

English translation found on page 109.

Original #11
July 22, 1926

トレド事件
公判第七日

公判の総結
漸く近づく

English translation found on page 113.

Original #12

October 1, 1926

トレド排日事件
被告損害を辨償し
判決に服した上に今後
日本人を排斥せぬと約束
他の訴訟取り下げ

[illegible]タ夫妻外数名を相手取り
[illegible]万弗の損害賠償訴訟は故タ
[illegible]ートン判事の公平なる裁断
により原告同胞側の勝訴となり
損害金として二千五百弗を支拂
ふべき旨の言ひ渡しありたるト
レド排日事件は被告側は此の訴
訟の爲め財産の殆ど全部を費消
し破産の状態にある由にて判決
后代理人ダリーン辨護士を通じ
て原告側辨護士タムソン氏に善意
の交渉あり日本人側は協議の結
果被告等は判決を承認し損害金
二千五百弗を支拂ふと共に今后
は同地へ日本人が入り込む場
合決して排斥或は抗議しないと
の條件を容れて事件は昨日午後
タムソン辨護士事務所に會合し
て落着した右事件は小倉玉吉氏
の名義の分にて同時に他の川本
同[illegible]、坪川、故三谷諸氏の
事件も被告等の誠意を認めて取
り下げることになつた

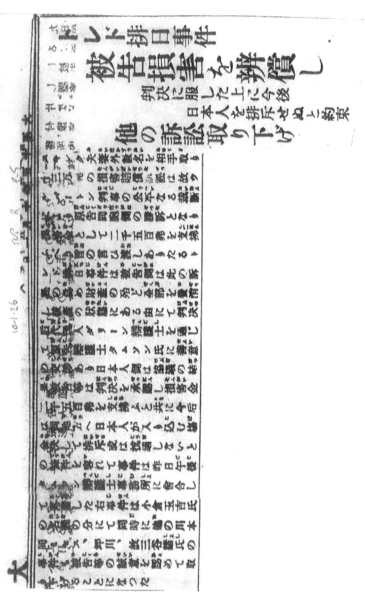

English translation found on page 124.

People Index

A
Adderson, Morris ... 52
Allen, George C. ... 45
Altree, Mamie ... 40,46,96
Amano, Matt ... xii
Anderson, Mrs. R. A. ... 27
Anderson, Maurice ... 84
Angillis, Donato ... 47
Amick, Glen-Paul ... ix,66,69,92,94,95,99,101,103,106,109,113,124,154
Amick, Hiroko ... ix,66,69,92,94,95,99,101,103,106,109,113,124,154

B
Baker, John H. ... viii
Banks, W.W. ... xiv
Bateman, Leo R ... 63
Bateman, Mrs. Ethel ... 27,63,110,111
Bean, Judge Robert S ... 125
Bennett, Roy ... xii
Boggs, Monte ... xi
Boardman, Howard P ... 122
Bolton, Lyall R. (1903-1989) ... 46
Bredstead, Chris ... 41,46,108
Brekke, Carl ... 63
Buck, Charles A ... 41,52,67,78,91
Burns, Mrs. James ... 46

C
Carson, Sonny ... 44
Castilla, Griselle Leclerc ... 196
Chambers, Fred ... 27
Chandler, Lynne ... xii
Chandler, Tom ... xii
Coffin, Chris. ... xii
Collier, Attorney John ... 91,92,95,98,101,102,106,107,111,112,113,114,116,117,118,155,157
Colvin, William S. (1875-1936) ... 37,38,41,47,48,49,52,67,78,91,99,111,112,115,122,125,126,127,155

Coman, Rosemary 148,149
Conrad, E. P 63,81,83,84
Cook. Lorena (1874-1936) 84
Cox, Ted .... iii,v, 196
Cox, Veronica O .... xii, 196
Currier, Ray xii

D
Daniels, Jess 49,50,52,99
Davis, R. H. 84
Day, Howard S. (Smitty) 52
Davis, Linda 196
Delzell, William A. 62, 107
Disque, Brice P. 7,8
Doyle, Suzanna xii
Dunham, E. H. 27
Dye, Patricia Sturdevant x,39,45.127

E
Emerson, L. D. 41,78,91

F
Ferris, Gordon 27
Fitzgerald, W. H 62
Fox, J. C 84
Francis, Dixie xii

G
Germer, Martin H 41,45,46,47,49,52,67,78,91,96,99
Gram, Charles H 62,69
Green, B. A 78,79,80,81,83,84,90,92,95,97,102, 114,115,117,122,123,124,125
Green, Allen (1887-1982) 62
Green, Bill 62
Green, Roy A. .... vii, x, 62, 196
Griswald, Arthur B. 41
Guardino, Connie vii,xi,39

H
Hall, G. W 39,107
Haller, Andrea xi
Harrison, Loretta xi

Harrington, Matt xii
Hart, Jerolea 151
Hart, LaRue x
Hart, Larry x,151
Hart, Owen v,41,44,45,46,53,78,91,96,98,108, 122,126,127,129,150,151,155
Hart, Rolland (Pug) xi
Hart, Rollie C 41,53,108,151
Hawkins, Harry xi,34,39
Hendrix, Guy x
Horning, Fred 52
Horsfall, George H. (1856-1939) 41,43,48,49,67,93,99
Hotchkiss, Clarence R. 78,126

I
Ide, W. G 23,64,68,136
Inskeep, J. H 38
Ito, Kazuo 125

J
Jacobson, A. 106,107
Jenkins, Martha xii
Johnson, A 78
Johnson, C. D 12,13,23,24,25,41,42,43,44,45, 49,51,67,68,78,84,99,112,149
Johnson, Dean 13,18,19,20,23,24,26,41,42,44,94,99
Johnson, Dean, III xi,24,25,41
Johnson, Mary xii
Johnson, Simon xii
Juntunen, Judy A. xii

K
Kawamoto, George 34,48
Kawamoto, Ichiro (1883-1975) 34,35,40,42,45,47,48,49, 50,51,53,77,81,82,94,99, 100,103,111,155
Kawamoto, Ito (1883-1950) 34,35,45,47,48,50,77,81, 98,99,116,124,155,156
Kawamoto, Kiyoshi 34,48
Kawamoto, Shizue (1923-1989) 34,48
Kessler, Lauren .... xii,xiv
Keyes, William 38

Kimmel, J. M. 38
Krause, Leonard...90,92,117

L
Laughlin, G. M 84
Leclerc, Mauricio A. 196
Lindsay, W. A 27

M
Macintyre, P. I. [sic] 109
Markham, John F 43,44,45,49
Martin, Lester...96
Marvin, Arthur E 110,111
Mathews, Celeste...xi,128,129,130
Matsler, Nik...xii
Matsui, Yorisada x
Matthews, William...96
Mclain Cheri xii
McMurray, Archer L..49,94
McNally, Betty ....vii,xii
McNary, Charles L. (Senator)..68,110
Mendoza, Rosa xi
Midzusawa, K 81
Miller, Lisa xi
Miller, Nels W 84
Mitani, Youjiro...53,77,81,124,155
Morris, C. (Reverend)..63,109

N
Namba, Etsuo 139
Namba, Kenji...139
Neal, Sid x,53,58,150

O
O'Day, Janet xii
O'Donnell, Mike..vii
Ogura, Tamakichi 34,35,40,50,51,53,77,81,99,115,
124,125,126,137,138,139,154,155,156
Okamoto, Hisakichi..27,64,72
Oyama, Albert x
Oyama, Iwao 72,73,74,147,148

P
Palmer, Lloyd M. xii,7
Parrish, George 52
Peterson, D. L 20
Pierce, Walter M xv,27,62,63,64,65,68,69,72,74,81
Plank, (Deputy) 48
Powers, Louis xi
Pratt, Harland L. 196
Pritchard, Harry T 27,36,37,41,42,44,45,52,63,78, 91,97,101,102,103,122,126,155

R
Rayment, Peter xi
Rehn, Linda xii
Richardson, Bob 46
Richardson, A.R. 45,46,49,52,115
Riggs, Inez 50
Roberts, Earl x,28
Roberts, Guy 8,9,14
Robeson, Jackie x,126,127
Román, Melissa xii
Ross, Fred 79,125,126
Ross, Verne 27,63
Rossman, (Chief Justice) 139

S
Schenck, Jack 91,149
Schenck, Rosemary 19,20,21,22,27,38,63,78,91,96, 97,110,111,112,113,115,122,125,126,127, 148,149,150,155
Schenck, George R. 19,35,50,52,53,78,91,107,113, 114,115,116,117,122,126,127, 148,149,155
Schick, Harry 128,129,130
Schumann, June x,147,148
Schlecht, H.A. 52
Smith, Doris 150
Smith, Sandy xii
Stack, Edward J 64,78,90
Stevens, Frank W 22,26,44,45,63
Stewart, James 52
Stokes, W. R 27

Sturdevant, Frank 41,78,91,122,126,127,155
Sturdevant, Margaret 127

T
Takeoka, Kay x,144,145,146
Takeoka, (Charles) Daiichi xii,80,81,82,144,145,146,147
Takemura, Eiji. ix
Tamura, Linda....................xii
Tanaka, Stefan.................... iii,iv,v,vi,viii,x
Tangen, Peter 48
Thompson, W. Lair 77,80,81,83,90,91,92,112,
116,117,123,124
Townsend, Peter....................115
Tindall, Lillian 27
Tsuboi, Masumi 155
Tsubokawa, Matsuto 77,81,155
Turner, R. M....................63,90,92,117,118

U
Uggen, John....................viii

V
Velie, John H. (1874-1931)....................23,24,26,146

W
Waugh, Alice....................27,63
Weeber, Jodi xi
Weller, Tom xii
Wessell, Joan....................xii
White, Carl R 112
Willis, Tim xi,137,138,139,140,144,145
Wirfs, Arthur M. (1894-1966) 51,53
Wirfs, Mrs. A. M....................50
Wisneiwski, Andrew (1894-1966)....................84
Wolverton, Charles Edwin (1851-1926)....................81,83,91,92,97,
101,102,106,112,118,
119, 122, 124,125,155
Wolcott, Jack xii
Woolfolk, Terry....................xii
Wyatt, Steve M vii

Y
Yamano, Kazu (1894-1950)....35,53
Yamano, Koichi (1881-1959)....35,53
Yasui, Homer....x,73,81,130,131,132,146
Yasui, Masuo....130
Yasui, Miki....v,73, 81,130,146
Yasui, Min....xv
Yoneyama, John T....98,126
Young, J. O....26

Subject Index

A
Affidavits....80,81,82,146
Air power 6
Aircraft
    airplanes....6,7,8,10,20
    DeHaviland bi-plane 6
    Production Board 7
Alien Land Law(s) 139,140,146
Aliens....iii,xiii,xvi,74,77,80,83,123, 135,137,138,139,140
Alsea Southern Railroad....3,13
American Federation of Labor (AFL)....xiii,xvi,87
American Legion....41
Archives
    National, Pacific AK Region, University of Washington....viii,78, 82,122
Armistice 11,12
Arrests 52
Asians 35,47,51
Attorney
    Corvallis....137,144
    Defense 63,78,79,80,81,83,84,90,92, 102,109,110,114,118,122, 123,124
    Lincoln County District Attorney 63,81,83,84
    Plaintiff 80,81,83,91,92,95,97,98, 101,102,103,106,107,108,109 111,112,113,114,115,116,117,118, 123,124,155,157

B
Bachelor 134
Baseball field (aka ballpark).... v,14,35,36,37,41,42,64,108
Black (see also Negro)....xiii,18,23,118,123,137
Bonds
    bail....80
    cost 80,81,83
Books
    Camp Adair viii
    Japan's Orient: Rendering Past Into History viii

New Times in Modern Japan viii
Issei:A History of Japanese Immigrants in North America 125
Boycott 63
Businessmen xv,23,24,26,39,64,67

C
California vi,viii,7,70,134,183
Northern California 7,70
Capacity, mill 14
Capitalists 105,106
Certificate of Registration 135
Chamber of Commerce
Land Settlement Department 64
Oregon 23,64,68,136
Toledo 18,19,23,68,73,109
Clallam County 7
Chinese 23,118
Citizens iv,xvi,4,22,36,54,63,64,75,79, 90,93,108,112,116,117,118, 123,125,126,131,134,136,137, 138,139,140,145,146
Citizenship xiii,134,146
Civil
lawsuit(s) (aka suits) viii,xi,xiii,63,76,77,81,83, 84,85,90,92-115, 123,128, 131,137,139,154-157
rights xi,xiii,77,78,123,128,131,137,139
Columbia County 54,80
Compensation 104,124,125
Conspiracy 116,117,118,119,137,138
Constitutions (U.S. and Oregon)
amendments to 137
racial biases of 138
Corvallis, Oregon vii,ix,xi,xvii,24,32,34,35,51, 52,53,54,68,73,76,83,84,91,94,108, 109,113,137,144,150,156
Cost bond 80,83
Court
Appellate 127,137,140
District iv,123
Council of Churches, Portland vii,74,75
Council of National Defense 7

Criminal
investigation 63,72,74,76,81,83
trial 83,85,118
Cross-examination 101,113,115

D
Damages 39,70,77,78,104,118,122,123,124
Defendants....................................78,79,80,83,85,90,91,92,94,96,97,
100,101,102,104,106,108,110,115,
117,122-127,154,155
Defense Attorney 80,89,109,110,114,117
Demonstration....................................39
Deportation vii,viii,ix,62,64,69,72,74,75,
83,117,127,128
Depositions....................................viii
Depot Slough....................................xix,2,10,14,41,42,98
Deputies. 44,45,48,49,50,52,67,78,
91,99,111,114,156
Discrimination xiv,xv,134,146

E
Editorial....................................8,38,54,69,103,106
Employees, mill 34,38,48,51,53,62,63,75,94,96,137,147
Equal protection 74,138,140
Evidence 81,85,95,104,112,113,118
Exclusion Act....................................139
Expulsion....................................iv,vii,ix,xiii,52,64,69,70,71,90

F
Federal Bureau of Investigation (FBI) 148
Fight....................................30,44,45,46,47,51,62,66,156
Filipino v,32,47,53,68,69
Fir and Spruce Lumber Co. xix,11
Firearm (aka; gun, handgun, revolver, pistol, weapon)..........xxi,
43-46, 49,51,
84,96,97,98
Fischer-Storey Sawmill....................................10
Flag
Stars and Stripes 41,45,46,47,49,54,
66,94,95,98,104,112
Foreman xx,34,37,40,42,77,111
Fourteenth Amendment 137,140

France 7,10
Fred Horning Transfer Company 52

G
Georgia Pacific Pulp and Paper Mill 42
Gempei War 71
Gentleman's Agreement 19,90,135
Germans 6
Globalization iv
Governor, Oregon xv,27,62-65,68,69,72,74,81, 101-104,107,110,156,157
Grand Jury....................................xxii,63,83,84,85
Great Britain 7,10
Green-chain xi,xix,18,19,20,22,24,25, 27,35,55,67,70,76,112, 123,129,130,136

H
Handbills 35,36
Handgun (aka; gun, firearm, revolver, pistol, weapon)..........xxi, 43-46,49,51,84,96,97,98
Harassment....................................35,51,72,95
Hasegawa Business Store....................................54,68
Highway 20 Business xix,4
Hindu 23
Housing....................................xx,xxi,3,14,19,21,28,30,32-35, 40-43,45-49,51,54,110,156

I
Immigration, 1924 Act .... xv, 136,139
Immigration, Japanese ii,xiii,xiv,xv,xvi,34,125, 134,135,136,139,144
Indictment 85
Interpreter 96,97,98,112
Invasion of property 90
Issei ii,iii,v,vi,ix,x,xi,xvi,18,26,27, 34,35,40,48,51-55,65,66,69, 72,73,75,76,77,80,81,83,90,93,98,100, 106,111,113,115,116,123,125,128, 134,135,136,145,146,147
Italy 7,10

J
Japan, country iii,xviii,20,26,64,90,134,135, 136,138,139,147,155,157
Japanese Ambassador 72
Consul..................................27,64,72,81,104,105,135,156
Japanese Association (of Oregon) ii,ix,x,23,26,73,74,76, 80,90,123,135,136,146
Ministry of Foreign Affairs 71,72
Japanese resident
Aliens ineligible for citizenship xiii
bachelors 134
baggage 47,51,52,54
Cultural Center x
Employment
Agency 23,136
Labor representative..................................23,62,69,78
in Oregon sawmills...............ii,10,112,123,131,136,137
Japantown (Nihonmachi) 147
Jobs xiv,xvi,3,7,8,9,10,18,20,22-25,27, 34,35,37,39,54,67-71, 75,76,80,90,112,118,119,123,124, 125,128,134,136,138,146,154,156,157
Judgment i,78,124,126
Jury xxii,63,83,84,85,92,98,115,117,118,119, 122,123,127,137,139,155

K
Korean v,32,53,68,69,103
Ku Klux Klan ....xv,xviii

L
Labor
advantages of..............................18,20,24,26,27,66,75,136
Farm Labor Legal Bureau 79,125,126
laborers iv,xiii,3,10,18,20,32,34,36,38, 39,40,41,48,53,54,64,67,68,69, 70,71,73,74,75,83,84,90,92,99,100, 105,106,109,110,134,156
language 65,144
newspapers....................................ii,ix,65,73,147,148,154
Oregon Bureau of Labor...ix,xiv
Oregon State Federation of Labor xiii,26,64,78,87,90

pay (wages)............................ iv,25,64,67,70,73,75,79,154
possessions 54
practices/culture of xiv
practicing law 144,145
railroad section labor 16,70,105
rights of......................ii,iii,v,xi,xiii,xvi,65,70,72,75,77,78,
79,81,93,100,123,128,137,138,
139,155,157
Secretary of Labor, Washington D.C............................112
State Deputy Labor Commissioner 62
State Labor Commissioner 62,69
transport for...32,52,54,112,113
Laborers, resident vs. non-resident................ xiv,3,4,18,136,138
Cook 35,77,156
Farm 35,77
Hop yards 34,77
Labor contract 32,34,99,100
Laundry 77
Lawyers, (attorneys).................... ii,xi,xv,63,77-81,83,84,90,92,
94,97,98,101,102,103,107-111,
113-116,118,122,123,124,127,137,
144,154,155,157
Defense 78,79,80,83,85,90,91,92,95,
97,98,100,101,104,106,107,109,
110,111,112,115,117
Japanese American xv
Lincoln County District Attorney 63,81,83,84
Plaintiff 80,81,91,92,97,102,106-109,
113-117,124,146,154,157
League of Women Voters xxi,76
Legal Fees 122,123
Lincoln County......................vii,xxii,3,7-10,12,14,15,21,32,36,
51,63,66,76,79,83,91,93,125,126
Grand Jury xxii,63,83,84,85
Lincoln County Protective League (LCPL).... iv,27,39,62-65,
78,79,101,106,
108,113,116
Little Tokyo (see Tokyo Slough) 3,34,54,116
Logging Camps 8,14,80
Logs...3,7,13,22
Lumber.......................................7,8,14,18,19,20,24,25,26,39

M
Magazines/publications
Bayfront Magazine vii
Pacific Northwest Quarterly .... v,vii
Oregon Voter ix,xxi,62,75,76
Management, mill 18,23,38,39,42,63
Marshal
City 19,35,50,52,53,62,74,78,113,116,117,149
United States 126
Mennonites 55,76
Merchant Hotel xxi,147,148
Merchants 26
Methodist Church 109
Military 6,8
Minority (minorities) 75,78,93,128,130,131,
Mob xiii,xx,23,39,41-52,54,63,64,66-72,74,
83,84,92-104,108,111,112,116-119,129,155,156
Mongolian xiii
Multnomah County 35,77,78,139

N
National Archives viii,78,82,122
Negro(es) xiii,23,118,123,137
Newport, Oregon xi,xix,xxii,3,4,16,38
Newspapers
Call Bulletin 149
Corvallis Gazette-Times 73
Great Northern Daily News (Taihoku Nippo) .... iv,ix,xxi,
65,66,69,92-95,98,99,101,103,105,
106,109,113,124,154,158
Lincoln County Leader xx,xxi,11,12,28,32,
36,38,39,125,148
Newport News vii,96
North American Times (Hokubei Jiji) 65
Morning Oregonian xviii,xix,12,27
Omaha Bee 149
Oregon Daily Journal 98,115,118,149
Oregon News (Oshu Nippo) ii,xxi,65,73,147,148
Oregon Nippo 148
Oregon Statesman 65
Portland Telegram 68
Yaquina Bay News 54

Nikkei viii,x,xvi,136,148
Nisei .... v,x,xvi
Non-resident 80

O
Olalla Slough 2,4
Oregon Bar Association 146
Oregon Coast History Center .... vii,xi
Oregon Constitution 138
Oregon Historical Society 130
Oregon Lung Association 148
Oregon Nikkei Legacy Center x,148
Oregon, State of
    Oregon State Legislature xiv,xv,139
    State Militia 38
Oregon State University 34,35,76,91
Oregon Supreme Court 139
Oregon Voter ix,xxi,62,75,76
Oriental Trading Company 70
Orientals iv,23,27,70,83,84,104,105,118
Oysters 22

P
Pacific Northwest Quarterly .... v,vii
Pacific Spruce Corporation i,iv,xi,xvi,xxi,xxii,3,14, 18,20-23,27,28,30,32,34,36,37,38, 41,51,54,55,62-68,72,73,74,76,77, 79,90,94,99,104,106,107,112,116, 117,118,122,123
    caféteria xix,21,23,24,26
    electric power plant 42
    Pacific Spruce Law Enforcement League 63
    payroll 13,14,15
Petition 27,80,156
Picture Bride 134
    Plaintiffs xxi,77,79,80,81,90,91,92, 94,95,97,98,99,102,103, 104,106-109,113-117, 122,124,138,146,154-157
Police xv,xx,35,62,67,70,75,103, 113,114,115,117,149
Population ix,xiii,xxii,13,14,34

Portland, Oregon iv,x,xiii,xx,xxi,13,23-27,34,35,53,54,
59,64-68,73,78,80,81,83,84,
90,91,92,94,95,104,106,109,113,
128,131,135,136,137,145-148,154,155
Portland Council of Churches viii,74
Portland Nikkei-Jin-Kai.. 136
Precedent, legal 3,77,79,127,138
Prejudice ix,75,118,138
Pritchard Mercantile Company 63
Property
taxes 21
title 21,126
values 20,37,126
Prosecution 63,77,81
Protest 19,23,25,41,76,92,110,112,124

R
Race relations 155
Racial
bias/prejudice ix,x,xiv,68,70,71,75,103,118,125,138
tension iv,40,49,66,67,71,72,90,103,111,115,118
Railroad xix,xx,3,7-11,13,14,16,32,33,40,
41,43,46,47,70,105
Rally xx,26,35-39,66,83,94,95,97,98,
101,102,104,107,116,117,156
Red Electric 54,59
Reporters ix,20,65,66,68,69,74,79,
95,98,106,107,123,154
Resident aliens ii,xiii,xiv,xv,xvi,20,65,71,72,73,
74,76,80,81,90,93,100,113,115,
118,137,138,139,146
Resistance 46,48,51,67
Resolutions 22,23,26,27
Retribution 62
Rights
civil ii,xi,xiii,78,123,128,132,137,139
treaty iii,72,90,92,118,138,155,157
violations 76,81,128
Riot vii,xx,44,45,46,51,52,54,55,
62,63,64,66,68,69,74,76,79,
100,110,114-117,131
Rioters 45,46,52

S
Salmon 22
Sawmills in Toledo
Altree Sawmill 8
Chesley Sawmill 8,9
Fischer-Storey Sawmill 10
Government sawmill 7-13
Guy Roberts Sawmill 8,9,14
Pacific Spruce Mill xi,23,28,32,36,51,73
Yaquina Bay Railroad and Lumber Company .... xix,xx, 7-11,32
Sawmills *Issei* worked in
Yaquina Bay Railroad and Lumber Company .... xix,xx, 7-11,32
See Appendix A, page 136
Sawmills, 1925 136,137
Scandinavian 25
School board 22
Security 55,63,67,70,75,138
Settlement, out-of-court 123,125,126,139
Shed Five xx,42,43,47,51
Sitka Spruce 6,7
fibers 7
lumber iii,xix,6,7,8,20,22,64
Production Division 7,9,10
wood xx,6,7,25
Soldier(s) xix,7-11,140
South Beach 3
Southern Pacific Railroad 3,32,40,43,47,54,59,
Corvallis Depot 54,113
Toledo Depot 30,32
Standard of living xiv,64,79
State Militia 38
Summons xxi,78,91
Swift & Company 145

T
Takatsugu Misao Hotel 54
Tax revenue 21
Telegram 112,113
Testimony 95-99,101-104,106,107,108,111,115,118
Threatening letter 85

Tideland 2,8,28
Tides 2,3,28
Timber industry 2,13
Tokyo Slough xx,xxi,2,3,14,30,33,34,41,42,43,47,49,51,54
Toledo, City of
    Chamber of Commerce 18,19,20,23,68,73,109
    Fire Department 150
    location 2,3,8
    Marshal (Chief of Police) 19,35,50,52,53,55,
        62,74,78,113-117,149
    Police Department xx,35,62,75,149
    population xxi,13,14
    residents xiii,37,76,78,104,105,115,117,118
Toledo Businessmen's League 18,23,68
Trains xx,11,30,32,48,54,59,68
    tickets 50,53
Translators ix
Treaty of Commerce and Navigation (1911-1939) iii,72,90,
    92,118,138,139,155,157
Trial
    civil i,viii,xiii,52,63,80,81,83,84,90
    costs 79,80,125,126
    criminal 83
Turlock, California 70

U
United States
    Army 7,10,139
    Congress xv,7,139,140
    Congressman 68,110
    Council of National Defense 7
    Government Sawmill 7,10
    Salvage sale 11,12
    Secretary of Labor 112
    Spruce Corporation 8
    Spruce Production Division 7,9,10
University of Oregon
    Law School 144
    Oregana (University of Oregon Yearbook) xxi,144

V
Vanport, Oregon 148

Verdict xiii,xxi,104,119,122,123,124,131.138,139
Violence..................... 39,71,84,100-103,105,107,110,115,118

W

Wages (pay).................. iv,25,35,64,67,70,73,74,75,79,134,154
Warplanes 6,7,8
Wars
    Civil War, post 137
    World War I xiv,6,11
    World War II v,xvii,139,149
Washington, State of 7,11,12,105,134
    Auburn 70
    Longview 137
    Port Angeles 7
    Seattle viii,ix,78,82
    Toledo 131
    Vancouver 7
    Water 21,22,28,33,149
    Waterfront...............................xix,10,14,38,39,42,63,156
Waterways 2,3
Witnesses 93-98,103,104,106,108-115
Women x,xv,34,35,40,48,49,50,53,72,75,
77,96,99,100,103,134,147,148

Y

Yaquina Bay 3
Yaquina Bay News...54
Yaquina City xx,16,32
Yaquina River xix,xxii,2,3,4,9,22,42

Photograph by Linda Davis - 2004

About the Author

Ted W. Cox was born in Eugene, Oregon in 1947.

He is a 1967 graduate of Chaffey Jr. College, Alta Loma, California. In 1969, he received his B.A. Degree from LaVerne College, LaVerne, California.

From 1969 to 1973, Ted was a Peace Corps Volunteer. For two years he taught at the Bo Teacher Training College in Sierra Leone, West Africa, followed by two years as the National Track and Field Coach of Belize, Central America.

Ted completed his Masters Degree in Education at Oregon State University, Corvallis, Oregon in 1975. While at OSU, he was head coach of the University Woman's Volleyball team in 1973 and 1974. From 1975 to 1976 he taught physical education and first aid at Linn-Benton Community College, Albany, Oregon.

Since 1977, he has owned and operated the Old World Deli in downtown Corvallis. For over twenty-five years his restaurant has been a center of daily gathering for local 'old timers' interested in history led by Mr. Harland Pratt.

Ted is married to Veronica. He has a daughter, Griselle, who is married and lives in Monterrey, Mexico and a son, Mauricio, who is married and lives in Portland, Oregon.

At the time of this publication, Ted is writing two history books; *The Life and Times of Roy Green: 1910-1945*, and *The Butter Tub Book: A History of Wooden Butter Tubs in America - 1882-1944.*